Daniel

THE
STAYING SOBER
WORKBOOK

EXERCISE
MANUAL

A Serious Solution for the Problem of Relapse

TERENCE T. GORSKI

Based Upon the CENAPS Model of Treatment

Independence Press
Independence, Missouri

THE STAYING SOBER WORKBOOK

Exercise Manual

Contents

THE STABILIZATION CHECKLIST
Instructions

Evaluate how well you function in each of these areas under both high and low stress. As you answer the questions keep the following definitions of high and low stress in mind:

High Stress: any situation in which you are agitated, under pressure, under close observation or a deadline, and/or which has the potential for conflict or problems between you and others

Low Stress: any situation in which you have low personal responsibility or investment, time constraints are minimal, and/or the outcome poses little threat to you or others

Check the box which is closest to your true feelings: always, usually, sometimes, or never. Place the score for that description on the blank line. At the end of the exercise add up all of your scores. The higher your score the less stable you are and the less able you will be to do relapse prevention planning right now. If your score is more than 40, do not do this workbook alone. You should seek professional counseling to help you become stabilized.

Ability to Think Clearly: *the ability to solve usually simple problems without becoming overwhelmed or confused*

1. I can solve usually simple problems without becoming overwhelmed or confused:
   A. under high stress

   ____ ☐ always (0)   ☐ usually (1)   ☐ sometimes (2)   ☐ never (4)

   B. under low stress

   ____ ☐ always (0)   ☐ usually (2)   ☐ sometimes (4)   ☐ never (8)

Ability to Manage Feelings and Emotions: *the ability to identify what you are feeling, react appropriately to those feelings and emotions (neither overreact or underreact), and communicate your feelings and emotions to others when it is appropriate to do so*

2. I am able to recognize my feelings and emotions:
   A. under high stress

   ____ ☐ always (0)   ☐ usually (1)   ☐ sometimes (2)   ☐ never (4)

   B. under low stress

   ____ ☐ always (0)   ☐ usually (2)   ☐ sometimes (4)   ☐ never (8)

3. My feelings and emotions are appropriate (I don't over or underreact) to the thoughts I am having or to the situation I am in:
   A. under high stress

   ____ ☐ always (0)   ☐ usually (1)   ☐ sometimes (2)   ☐ never (4)

   B. under low stress

   ____ ☐ always (0)   ☐ usually (2)   ☐ sometimes (4)   ☐ never (8)

4. I am able to tell other people what I am feeling when it is appropriate or important to do so:
   A. under high stress

   ____ ☐ always (0)   ☐ usually (1)   ☐ sometimes (2)   ☐ never (4)

   B. under low stress

   ____ ☐ always (0)   ☐ usually (2)   ☐ sometimes (4)   ☐ never (8)

Ability to Remember

5. I can usually remember what has recently happened to me and remember appointments and arrangements:
   A. under high stress

   _____ ☐ always (0)   ☒ usually (1)   ☐ sometimes (2)   ☐ never (4)

   B. under low stress

   _____ ☐ always (0)   ☐ usually (2)   ☐ sometimes (4)   ☐ never (8)

Ability to Exercise Good Judgment

6. I can usually predict the logical consequences of my own behavior:
   A. under high stress

   _____ ☒ always (0)   ☐ usually (1)   ☐ sometimes (2)   ☐ never (4)

   B. under low stress

   _____ ☐ always (0)   ☐ usually (2)   ☐ sometimes (4)   ☐ never (8)

7. I can usually predict the logical consequences of other people's behavior:
   A. under high stress

   _____ ☐ always (0)   ☐ usually (1)   ☐ sometimes (2)   ☐ never (4)

   B. under low stress

   _____ ☐ always (0)   ☐ usually (2)   ☐ sometimes (4)   ☐ never (8)

8. I can usually predict the logical consequences of important situations or events that occur in my life:
   A. under high stress

   _____ ☐ always (0)   ☐ usually (1)   ☐ sometimes (2)   ☐ never (4)

   B. under low stress

   _____ ☐ always (0)   ☐ usually (2)   ☐ sometimes (4)   ☐ never (8)

Ability to Control Behavior

9. I take appropriate action based upon my judgment and do what I say to myself I need to do:
   A. under high stress

   _____ ☐ always (0)   ☐ usually (1)   ☐ sometimes (2)   ☐ never (4)

   B. under low stress

   _____ ☐ always (0)   ☐ usually (2)   ☐ sometimes (4)   ☐ never (8)

10. I refrain from doing what I know is not in my best interest in spite of urges or compulsions to do so:
    A. under high stress

    _____ ☐ always (0)   ☐ usually (1)   ☐ sometimes (2)   ☐ never (4)

    B. under low stress

    _____ ☐ always (0)   ☐ usually (2)   ☐ sometimes (4)   ☐ never (8)

Total Score: _____ *(add all your scores from each part)*

The Staying Sober Workbook by Terence T. Gorski
Available from: Independence Press, P.O. Box HH, Independence, MO 64055

Name: _____

THE WEEKLY EVALUATION OF INTERNAL FUNCTIONING

For the week starting _____ **and ending** _____

1. Difficulty in thinking clearly	A.	B.	C.
A. Inability to concentrate for more than a few minutes			
B. Inability to solve usually simple problems			
C. Rigid and repetitive thinking			
D. Abstract thinking			
E. Thinking logically			
F. Understanding cause/effect relationships			
G. Setting priorities			

2. Difficulty in managing feelings and emotions	A.	B.	C.
A. Overreacting emotionally			
B. Feeling emotionally numb			
C. Having strong feelings for no reason			
D. Mood swings			
E. Depression			
F. Strong fear/anxiety			
G. Strong anger/resentment			

3. Difficulty in remembering	A.	B.	C.
A. Forgetting things within 20 minutes			
B. Forgetting new skills			
C. Not remembering important childhood events			
D. Not remembering important adulthood events			

Scoring Key

A
How often did it occur?

0. Did not occur
1. Once during the week
2. Several times during the week
3. Once a day
4. More than once a day
5. Don't know

B
How long did it last?

0. Did not occur
1. Less than 15 minutes
2. 15 minutes to 1 hour
4. 7 to 23 hours
5. 1 to 3 days
6. 4 to 7 days
7. Don't know

C
How disruptive was it?

0. Did not occur
1. Not at all; able to perform normal acts of daily living (ADL) without extra effort
2. Mildly disruptive; able to perform ADL but had to expend extra effort to do so
3. Moderately disruptive; unable to perform some ADL some of the time in spite of extra effort
4. Severely disruptive; unable to perform many ADL much of the time in spite of efforts

4. Difficulty with physical coordination	A.	B.	C.
A. Dizziness			
B. Trouble with balance			
C. Hand-eye coordination problems			
D. Slow reflexes			
E. Clumsiness			
F. Accident proneness			

5. Difficulty in sleeping	A.	B.	C.
A. Difficulty falling asleep			
B. Unusual or disturbing dreams			
C. Awaking many times during the night			
D. Not being rested after sleeping			
E. Always feeling tired			
F. Changes in time of day when sleep occurs			
G. Sleeping for extremely long periods			

6. Difficulty managing stress	A.	B.	C.
A. Inability to recognize minor signs of stress			
B. Inability to relax when stress is recognized			
C. Constant fatigue			
D. Fear of physical collapse due to stress			
E. Fear of mental collapse due to stress			
F. Inability to function normally due to severe stress			

7. Please describe what you did during the course of the week to manage these symptoms.

_____

_____

Scoring Key

A
How often did it occur?

0. Did not occur
1. Once during the week
2. Several times during the week
3. Once a day
4. More than once a day
5. Don't know

B
How long did it last?

0. Did not occur
1. Less than 15 minutes
2. 15 minutes to 1 hour
4. 7 to 23 hours
5. 1 to 3 days
6. 4 to 7 days
7. Don't know

C
How disruptive was it?

0. Did not occur
1. Not at all; able to perform normal acts of daily living (ADL) without extra effort
2. Mildly disruptive; able to perform ADL but had to expend extra effort to do so
3. Moderately disruptive; unable to perform some ADL some of the time in spite of extra effort
4. Severely disruptive; unable to perform many ADL much of the time in spite of efforts

THE SELF-ASSESSMENT OF TREATMENT NEED

Instructions

This exercise will help you determine if you have completed the basic tasks of recovery in your previous efforts to stay sober. Your composite score will tell you if you need AA plus basic counseling, AA plus relapse prevention counseling, or AA plus both basic and relapse prevention counseling.

Choose the most appropriate answer to each question. At the end of each choice is a number from 0 to 5.

Write that number on the line in front of each question. Some questions ask you to check two separate responses. In these cases the score for the second question is always 0.

Add your total score and see where it fits on the chart. If you have any questions seek the help of a certified alcohol or drug abuse counselor.

Section I: Past Efforts at Sobriety and Treatment

_____ 1. I have attempted long-term sobriety on at least one previous occasion and managed to maintain at least _____ weeks of abstinence.

  ☐ 12 weeks (4)

  ☐ 6 weeks (3)

  ☐ 4 weeks (2)

  ☐ less than 4 weeks (1)

  ☐ I have never attempted long-term sobriety (0)

_____ 2. I have been admitted to a short term (3–10 day) detoxification program _____ times and have left before completing the program _____ times.

  A. Number of times admitted

  ☐ three or more times (3)

  ☐ twice (2)

  ☐ once (1)

  ☐ never (0)

  B. Number of times left before completing

  ☐ three or more (0)

  ☐ twice (0)

  ☐ once (0)

  ☐ never (0)

_____ 3. I have been admitted to a residential (inpatient) rehabilitation program for alcoholism/drug specific treatment _____ times and have left before completing the program _____ times.

  A. Number of times admitted

  ☐ three or more times (3)

  ☐ twice (2)

  ☐ once (1)

  ☐ never (0)

  B. Number of times left before completing

  ☐ three or more (0)

  ☐ twice (0)

  ☐ once (0)

  ☐ never (0)

_____ 4. I have been previously treated in an _outpatient_ alcoholism/drug specific treatment center.

  A. Number of times admitted

  ☐ three or more times (3)

  ☐ twice (2)

  ☐ once (1)

  ☐ never (0)

  B. Number of times left before completing

  ☐ three or more (0)

  ☐ twice (0)

  ☐ once (0)

  ☐ never (0)

During efforts at recovery people vary in their level of involvement. Think of the time when you were most actively involved in your recovery while you answer the following questions.

_____ 5. When I was most actively involved in my recovery I typically attended _____ Twelve Step (AA, NA, etc.) meetings per week.

  ☐ 3 meetings per week (4)

  ☐ 2 meetings per week (3)

  ☐ 1 meeting per week (2)

  ☐ less than 1 meeting per week (1)

  ☐ I have never attended Twelve Step meetings (0)

_____ 6. When I was most actively involved in my recovery I participated in conversations with other recovering people, outside of AA or therapy meetings, _____ times per week.

  ☐ 7 or more times per week (3)

  ☐ 3–6 times per week (2)

  ☐ 1–2 times per week (1)

  ☐ less than once per week (0)

_____ 7. When I was most actively involved in my recovery I did a review and evaluation of daily problems and activities (a tenth-step inventory), outside of AA or therapy meetings, _____ times per week.

  ☐ 7 or more times per week (3)

  ☐ 3–6 times per week (2)

  ☐ 1–2 times per week (1)

  ☐ less than once per week (0)

_____ 8. When I was most actively involved in my recovery I read or listened to tapes of recovery-oriented literature or speakers, outside of AA and therapy meetings, _____ times per week.

  ☐ 7 or more times per week (3)

  ☐ 3–6 times per week (2)

  ☐ 1–2 times per week (1)

  ☐ less than once per week (0)

_____ 9. When I was most actively involved in my recovery I talked with my Twelve Step Program sponsor, outside of AA or therapy meetings, _____ times per week.

  ☐ 7 or more times per week (3)

  ☐ 3–6 times per week (2)

  ☐ 1–2 times per week (1)

  ☐ less than once per week (0)

_____ 10. I completed a formal written Fourth and Fifth Step with my Twelve Step Program sponsor or other long-term sober member of my self-help group.

  ☐ completed written Fourth Step and Fifth Step (3)

  ☐ completed written Fourth Step but did not do a Fifth Step (2)

  ☐ did a Fourth Step in my mind but never wrote it down or talked with anyone about it (1)

  ☐ never did a Fourth or Fifth Step (0)

_____ 11. When I relapsed, I began using alcohol/drugs _____ weeks after my last attendance at a Twelve Step meeting.

☐ less than one (4)

☐ one to three (3)

☐ four to seven (2)

☐ eight or more (1)

_____ 12. The longest time period that I have been continuously involved in treatment through an outpatient/aftercare program has been _____ weeks.

☐ sixteen or more (4)

☐ nine to sixteen (3)

☐ five to eight (2)

☐ one to four (1)

☐ I have never attended an outpatient/aftercare program. (0)

_____ 13. When I was most involved in an outpatient/aftercare program, I attended group therapy meetings _____ times per month.

☐ ten or more (4)

☐ six to eight (3)

☐ two to five (2)

☐ less than two (1)

☐ I have never attended an outpatient/aftercare program. (0)

_____ 14. When I was most involved in an outpatient/aftercare program, I attended individual therapy meetings _____ times per month.

☐ ten or more (4)

☐ six to eight (3)

☐ two to five (2)

☐ less than two (1)

☐ I have never attended an outpatient/aftercare program. (0)

Section II: Recognition and Acceptance of Chemical Dependency

_____ 15. I understand and I am able to discuss the basic information about addictive disease.

☐ I can explain it clearly to others without help. (3)

☐ I can explain it clearly to others with help. (2)

☐ I understand it but cannot explain it. (1)

☐ I do not understand it. (0)

_____ 16. I believe in my own mind that I am suffering from addictive disease (alcoholism or other drug addictions).

☐ totally convinced (3)

☐ mostly convinced (2)

☐ partially convinced (1)

☐ not convinced (0)

_____ 17. When I think about my addiction (alcoholism or drug dependence) I experience the following level of inner conflict or pain _____:

☐ no inner conflict when thinking or talking about addiction (3)

☐ mild discomfort when talking about it (2)

☐ serious discomfort when talking about it (1)

☐ so uncomfortable I refuse to talk about it (0)

Section III: Evidence of Past Relapse Warning Signs

_____ 18. I am currently sober and experiencing pain or dysfunction.

☐ Yes, and I fear that I may relapse soon. (3)

☐ Yes, and I have some concern about relapse. (1)

☐ Yes, but I am not in immediate danger of relapse but want to lower my risk. (0)

☐ No, I am not currently experiencing pain or dysfunction and am not concerned about the immediate risk of relapse. (0)

_____ 19. In the past I have experienced episodes of pain or dysfunction when abstinent from alcohol or drugs that:

☐ caused me to use alcohol or drugs in spite of my honest desire not to. (3)

☐ caused me to feel a compulsion to use alcohol and drugs in spite of my honest desire not to but I did not use. (2)

☐ caused me to think about using alcohol and drugs without feeling a compulsion, and I did not use. (1)

☐ I never experienced episodes of dysfunction. (0)

_____ 20. In the past I have experienced progressive problems while abstinent from alcohol and drugs that caused me to think about using alcohol or drugs for relief.

☐ Yes, and it caused me to use alcohol or drugs in spite of my honest desire not to. (3)

☐ Yes, and it caused me to feel a compulsion to use alcohol and drugs in spite of my honest desire not to but I did not use. (2)

☐ Yes, and it caused me to think about using alcohol and drugs without feeling a compulsion, and I did not use. (1)

☐ I never experienced progressive problems. (0)

The chart below will help you determine whether you need basic treatment (with AA) for your alcohol or drug use, whether you need relapse prevention planning (with AA), or whether you need all of them.

Total Score: _____
0–18: Basic Treatment and AA
19–43: Relapse Prevention Planning, AA, and Basic Counseling
44–66: Relapse Prevention Planning and AA

The Staying Sober Workbook by Terence T. Gorski
Available from: Independence Press, P.O. Box HH, Independence, MO 64055

Name: _____

THE RELAPSE CALENDAR
Developed by Terence T. Gorski

Year:	January	February	March	April	May	June	July	August	September	October	November	December

The Staying Sober Workbook by Terence T. Gorski
Available from: Independence Press, P.O. Box HH, Independence, MO 64055

Name: _____

THE RELAPSE CALENDAR
Developed by Terence T. Gorski

Year:	January	February	March	April	May	June	July	August	September	October	November	December

The Staying Sober Workbook by Terence T. Gorski
Available from: Independence Press, P.O. Box HH, Independence, MO 64055

Exercise 5

THE RELAPSE EPISODE LISTS

My initial sobriety date is _____.

No.		Start		End		Duration	Function Level	
		MO	YR	MO	YR		High	Low
	Period of Abstinence:							
1	Relapse Episode:							

No.		Start		End		Duration	Function Level	
		MO	YR	MO	YR		High	Low
	Period of Abstinence:							
2	Relapse Episode:							

No.		Start		End		Duration	Function Level	
		MO	YR	MO	YR		High	Low
	Period of Abstinence:							
3	Relapse Episode:							

No.		Start		End		Duration	Function Level	
		MO	YR	MO	YR		High	Low
	Period of Abstinence:							
4	Relapse Episode:							

No.		Start		End		Duration	Function Level	
		MO	YR	MO	YR		High	Low
	Period of Abstinence:							
5	Relapse Episode:							

The Staying Sober Workbook by Terence T. Gorski
Available from: Independence Press, P.O. Box HH, Independence, MO 64055

		Start		End		Duration	Function Level	
		MO	YR	MO	YR		High	Low
No.	Period of Abstinence:							
6	Relapse Episode:							

		Start		End		Duration	Function Level	
		MO	YR	MO	YR		High	Low
No.	Period of Abstinence:							
7	Relapse Episode:							

		Start		End		Duration	Function Level	
		MO	YR	MO	YR		High	Low
No.	Period of Abstinence:							
8	Relapse Episode:							

		Start		End		Duration	Function Level	
		MO	YR	MO	YR		High	Low
No.	Period of Abstinence:							
9	Relapse Episode:							

		Start		End		Duration	Function Level	
		MO	YR	MO	YR		High	Low
No.	Period of Abstinence:							
10	Relapse Episode:							

Level of Function Scale

Description:	Score:	Criteria:
Excellent	10 or 9	—I can usually function well and it usually takes little or no effort.
Very Good	8 or 7	—I can usually function well but sometimes it requires extra effort.
Good	6 or 5	—I can usually function well but it almost always requires extra effort.
Fair	4 or 3	—I can only function well some of the time even with extra effort.
Poor	1 or 2	—I can seldom function well even with extra effort.
Very Poor	0	—I can almost never function well even with extra effort.

THE ASSESSMENT OF RECOVERY

Instructions

Think of your first period of abstinence. Read each question below and enter the letter of the correct answer in the box under "Period of Abstinence 1." Choose the answer that fits best for that period of abstinence. Think of your next period of abstinence and repeat the procedure until you have answered the questions for all past periods of abstinence.

1. Pretreatment: During the _____ period of abstinence...
   (Select only one)
   A. I believed that after a period of abstinence I would be able to return to the controlled use of alcohol or other drugs.
   B. I began to doubt my ability to control my alcohol or drug use.
   C. I knew for a fact, with little or no doubt in my mind, that I could not control my alcohol or drug use.

Period of Abstinence:

Answer for Each
Period of Abstinence

1	2	3	4	5	6	7	8	9	10

2. Stabilization: During the _____ period of abstinence...
   (Select only one)
   A. I never regained the ability to think clearly, manage my feelings and emotions, accurately remember things, exercise good judgment, and consistently manage my own behavior.
   B. I was sometimes able to control my thinking, feelings and emotions, memory, judgment and behavior, and at other times I couldn't.
   C. I was able to think clearly, manage my feelings and emotions, accurately remember things, exercise good judgment, and manage my own behavior most of the time.

Period of Abstinence:

Answer for Each
Period of Abstinence

1	2	3	4	5	6	7	8	9	10

3. Early Recovery: During the _____ period of abstinence...
   (Select only one)
   A. I never resolved my inner conflict about my chemical dependence.
   B. At times I felt my inner conflict about my chemical dependency was resolved, but at other times the conflicts would return.
   C. I fully resolved my inner conflicts about being chemically dependent and those conflicts never resurfaced while I was sober.

Period of Abstinence:

Answer for Each
Period of Abstinence

1	2	3	4	5	6	7	8	9	10

4. Middle Recovery: During the _____ period of abstinence...
   (Select only one)
   A. I never balanced out my life by fully repairing my relationships at home, work, and with friends.
   B. I started to balance my life by repairing my relationships at home, work, and with friends, but I found myself unable to fully repair past damage and develop satisfying new relationships.
   C. I fully balanced my life by repairing my relationships at home, work and with friends and by establishing new and satisfying relationships.

Period of Abstinence:

Answer for Each
Period of Abstinence

1	2	3	4	5	6	7	8	9	10

5. Late Recovery: During the _____ period of abstinence...
   (Select only one)
   A. I never examined or resolved any problems that I may have developed as a result of growing up in my family of origin.
   B. I recognized I had some family of origin problems but was never able to resolve them even though I tried to.
   C. I was able to identify and fully resolve the problems I had because of growing up in my family of origin.

Period of Abstinence:	1	2	3	4	5	6	7	8	9	10
Answer for Each Period of Abstinence										

6. Maintenance: During the _____ period of abstinence...
   (Select only one)
   A. I resolved all major problems with my recovery and felt I could stop working at ongoing growth and development.
   B. I resolved all major problems with my recovery and worked at ongoing growth and development but periodically became bored and complacent.
   C. I resolved all major problems with my recovery and continued with an active program of ongoing growth and development that I found interesting and exciting.

Period of Abstinence:	1	2	3	4	5	6	7	8	9	10
Answer for Each Period of Abstinence										

7. Have you made any progress in your recovery since you first attempted to stay abstinent?

   ☐ Yes.   ☐ No.   ☐ Unsure.

8. Please describe what you learned by completing this exercise.

_____

_____

_____

_____

_____

_____

_____

_____

_____

_____

_____

_____

_____

_____

The Staying Sober Workbook by Terence T. Gorski
Available from: Independence Press, P.O. Box HH, Independence, MO 64055

THE EXTERNAL CAUSES OF RELAPSE:

EXTERNAL CAUSES OF RELAPSE: An external cause of relapse is any problems with other people or situations that you have experienced outside of yourself while abstinent. A situation is defined as any problem or circumstance that you are involved with that does not include dealing with other people.

While abstinent before the most recent relapse episode:

A. Problems With Other People.

1. _____
2. _____
3. _____
4. _____
5. _____

B. Problems With Situations.

1. _____
2. _____
3. _____
4. _____
5. _____

While abstinent before the second most recent relapse episode:

A. Problems With Other People.

1. _____
2. _____
3. _____
4. _____
5. _____

B. Problems With Situations.

1. _____
2. _____
3. _____
4. _____
5. _____

While abstinent before the third most recent relapse episode:

A. Problems With Other People.

1. _____
2. _____
3. _____
4. _____
5. _____

B. Problems With Situations.

1. _____
2. _____
3. _____
4. _____
5. _____

Factors common to all three episodes:

1. _____
2. _____
3. _____

1. _____
2. _____
3. _____

The Staying Sober Workbook by Terence T. Gorski
Available from: Independence Press, P.O. Box HH, Independence, MO 64055

THE INTERNAL CAUSES OF RELAPSE:

INTERNAL CAUSES OF RELAPSE: An internal cause of relapse is any problem that you have experienced within yourself that does not involve interaction with other people or direct involvement with situations. The most common internal causes of relapse include both feelings and emotions and physical pain or illness.

While abstinent before the most recent relapse episode:

A. Feelings and Emotions.   B. Physical Pain or Illness.

1. _____   1. _____

2. _____   2. _____

3. _____   3. _____

4. _____   4. _____

5. _____   5. _____

While abstinent before the second most recent relapse episode:

A. Feelings and Emotions.   B. Physical Pain or Illness.

1. _____   1. _____

2. _____   2. _____

3. _____   3. _____

4. _____   4. _____

5. _____   5. _____

While abstinent before the third most recent relapse episode:

A. Feelings and Emotions.   B. Physical Pain or Illness.

1. _____   1. _____

2. _____   2. _____

3. _____   3. _____

4. _____   4. _____

5. _____   5. _____

Factors common to all three episodes:

1. _____   1. _____

2. _____   2. _____

3. _____   3. _____

The Staying Sober Workbook by Terence T. Gorski
Available from: Independence Press, P.O. Box HH, Independence, MO 64055

Exercise 9   **Name:** _____

THE COMBINED CAUSES OF RELAPSE

One of the major themes of this workbook is that relapse is always preceded by a sequence of warning signs. With help you can learn to recognize these warning signs and take action to stop them before they begin. To do this you will need to start thinking about the general steps that typically lead up to a relapse. These steps can be thought of as following rules, or laws, or principles. If you do certain things it sets you up to relapse. If you do other things it sets you up to recovery. Most people find they follow the same steps, with slight variation, before each relapse. This exercise is designed to help you start looking for the pattern that sets you up to relapse. If you can't find it now, don't worry about it. There are more exercises that follow to help you identify and clarify the pattern of set-up thoughts and behaviors.

Review the list of external and internal warning signs for all three relapse episodes. See if you can identify a general series of steps that you went through before you began using alcohol or drugs. Write those steps below. If you are not sure, guess at what they might be. Review these forms with your counselor and sponsor and tell them the steps to relapse that you discovered. Ask if they see anything that you missed.

THE STEPS TO ALCOHOL AND DRUG USE
MY FIRST ATTEMPT AT IDENTIFYING RELAPSE WARNING SIGNS

STEP 1: _____

_____

_____

STEP 2: _____

_____

_____

STEP 3: _____

_____

_____

STEP 4: _____

_____

_____

STEP 5: _____

_____

_____

_____

The Staying Sober Workbook by Terence T. Gorski
Available from: Independence Press, P.O. Box HH, Independence, MO 64055

Name: _____

RELAPSE EDUCATION SELF-TEST

(Developed by Merlene Miller)

INSTRUCTIONS: The following questions will help you test your understanding about relapse and relapse prevention planning. The numbers at the end of each question refer to the page in **Staying Sober** where you can find that particular information. Read those pages if you do not know the answer to any question or are unsure of any answer.

Part 1: Addictive Disease

1. Addiction is a condition in which a person develops dependence on any mood-altering substance.

   True _____   False _____   (39)

2. The pain of withdrawal is entirely psychological.

   True _____   False _____   (43)

3. High tolerance is an indication that a person is not addicted.

   True _____   False _____   (44)

4. The most effective treatment for alcoholism is Alcoholics Anonymous coupled with professional counseling.

   True _____   False _____   (52)

Part 2: Post Acute Withdrawal

5. Post acute withdrawal occurs before an addicted person goes through the acute abstinence syndrome.

   True _____   False _____   (57)

6. Post acute withdrawal is bio-psycho-social.

   True _____   False _____   (58)

7. Damage to the body and nervous system done by addiction contributes to post acute withdrawal.

   True _____   False _____   (58)

8. Forgetting something you learned 20 minutes before may be a symptom of post acute withdrawal.

   True _____   False _____   (60)

9. Even when sober, a recovering person may experience problems getting the right amount of sleep.

   True _____   False _____   (62)

10. At times of high stress, the symptoms of post acute withdrawal may become worse.

    True _____   False _____   (63)

11. Recovering persons can become unable to recognize and honestly tell others what they are thinking and feeling.

    True _____   False _____   (61)

Part 3: Managing Post Acute Withdrawal

12. Poor nutrition and inadequate exercise can create high-risk conditions for a post acute withdrawal episode.

    True _____   False _____   (73)

13. Caffeine is a natural stress reducer.

    True _____   False _____   (74) (118)

14. Sweets can prevent symptoms of post acute withdrawal from occurring.

    True _____   False _____   (74)

15. Relaxation exercises can help prevent post acute withdrawal symptoms.

    True _____   False _____   (77, 78)

16. Relaxation exercises cannot reduce already existing post acute withdrawal symptoms.

    True _____   False _____   (77, 78)

17. Laughing and daydreaming are examples of natural stress reducers.

    True _____   False _____   (77)

Part 4: Phases of Recovery

18. Pretreatment is the period of recovery when a person tests his or her ability to control alcohol and drug use.

    True _____   False _____   (85)

19. Stabilization includes recovery from the severe symptoms of post acute withdrawal.

    True _____   False _____   (87)

20. Early recovery is a time to recover from post acute withdrawal.

    True _____   False _____   (87)

21. Middle recovery is a time to learn how not to use drugs.

    True _____   False _____   (89)

22. Late recovery is a time for personality change.

    True _____   False _____   (90)

23. One task of the maintenance phase of recovery is watching for relapse warning signs.

    True _____   False _____   (93)

24. Partial recovery means you have failed to go to ninety meetings in ninety days.

    True _____   False _____   (93)

Part 5: The Relapse Syndrome

25. Relapse is a process.

    True _____   False _____   (124)

26. There are warning signs that occur long before addictive use begins.

    True _____   False _____   (130)

27. The symptoms of relapse develop subconsciously.

    True _____   False _____   (131)

28. The relapse syndrome usually begins with a breakdown in social structure.

    True _____   False _____   (132)

29. If you have admitted you are an alcoholic you have overcome denial.

    True _____   False _____   (125)

30. A change in thinking and feeling results in a change in behavior.

    True _____   False _____   (132)

The correct answers are listed in Appendix A at the end of this exercise manual.

The Staying Sober Workbook by Terence T. Gorski
Available from: Independence Press, P.O. Box HH, Independence, MO 64055

Name: _____

Date: _____

THE REVIEW OF RELAPSE WARNING SIGNS

As you review the following list of relapse warning signs:

—put a check by any warning sign that you have experienced;

—put a question mark if you have difficulty understanding what the warning sign means;

—put an asterisk (*) if you "space out" or begin daydreaming while reading the warning sign.

Phase I: Internal Warning Signs of Relapse. During this phase recovering people experience the inability to function normally within themselves. The most common symptoms are:

☐ **1–1. Difficulty in thinking clearly.** Recovering people often have trouble thinking clearly or solving usually simple problems. At times their minds race with rigid and repetitive thoughts. At other times their minds seem to shut off or go blank. They have difficulty concentrating or thinking logically for more than a few minutes. As a result they are not always sure about how one thing relates to or affects other things. They also have difficulty deciding what to do next in order to manage their lives and recovery. At times they are unable to think clearly and tend to make bad decisions that they would not have made if their thinking was normal.

☐ **1–2. Difficulty in managing feelings and emotions.** During periods of recovery many recovering people, at times, have difficulty in managing their feelings and emotions. At times they overreact emotionally (feel too much). At other times they become emotionally numb (feel too little) and are unable to know what they are feeling. At still other times they feel strange or "crazy feelings" for no apparent reason (feel the wrong thing) and may think they are going crazy. These problems in managing feelings and emotions have caused them to experience mood swings, depression, anxiety, and fear. As a result of this, they don't trust their feelings and emotions and often try to ignore, stuff, or forget about them. At times the inability to manage feelings and emotions has caused them to react in ways that they would not have acted if their feelings and emotions were properly managed.

☐ **1–3. Difficulty in remembering things.**

Many recovering people have memory problems that prevent them from learning new information and skills. The new things they learn tend to dissolve or evaporate from their mind within twenty minutes of learning them. They also have problems remembering key events from their childhood, adolescence, or adulthood. At times they remember things clearly. At other times these same memories will not come to mind. They feel blocked, stuck, or cut off from these memories. At times the inability to remember things has caused them to make bad decisions that they would not have made if their memory were working properly.

☐ **1–4. Difficulty in managing stress.** Many recovering people have difficulty in managing stress. They cannot recognize the minor signs of daily stress. When they do recognize the stress they are unable to relax. The things other people do to relax either don't work for them or make the stress worse. It seems they become so tense that they are not in control of it. As a result of this constant tension there are days when the strain becomes so severe they are unable to function normally and feel about to collapse physically or emotionally.

☐ **1–5. Difficulty in sleeping restfully.** During periods of recovery many recovering people have difficulty sleeping restfully. They cannot fall asleep. When they do sleep they have unusual or disturbing dreams. They awaken many times and have difficulty falling back asleep. They sleep fitfully and rarely experience a deep relaxing sleep. They awaken from a night of sleep feeling tired and not rested. The times of day at which they sleep change. At times they stay up late due to an inability to fall asleep and then oversleep because they are too tired to get up in the morning. At times they become so exhausted they sleep for extremely long periods, sometimes sleeping around the clock for one or more days.

☐ 1-6. *Difficulty with physical coordination and accidents.* During periods of recovery many recovering people have had difficulty with physical coordination that results in dizziness, trouble with balance, difficulty with hand-eye coordination, or slow reflexes. These problems create clumsiness and accident proneness that cause other problems they would not have had if their coordination were normal.

☐ 1-7. *Shame, guilt, and hopelessness.* At times many recovering people feel a deep sense of shame because they believe they are crazy, emotionally disturbed, defective as a person, or incapable of being or feeling normal. At other times they feel guilty because they believe they are doing something wrong or failing to work a proper recovery program. The shame and guilt cause them to hide the warning signs and stop talking honestly with others about what they are experiencing. The longer they keep them hidden the stronger the warning signs become. They try to manage these warning signs but fail. As a result they begin to believe that they are hopeless.

Phase II: Return of Denial. During this phase recovering people become unable to recognize and honestly tell others what they are thinking or feeling. The most common symptoms are:

☐ 2-1. *Concern About Well Being.* The internal warning signs of relapse make many recovering people feel uneasy, afraid and anxious. At times they may be afraid of not being able to stay sober. This uneasiness comes and goes and usually lasts only a short time.

☐ 2-2. *Denial of the Concern.* In order to tolerate these periods of worry, fear, and anxiety, they may ignore or deny these feelings in the same way they at one time denied addiction. The denial may be so strong that they are not aware of it while it is happening. Even when they are aware of the feelings, they are often forgotten as soon as they are gone. It is only when they think back about the situation at a later time that they are able to recognize the feelings of anxiety and the denial of those feelings.

Phase III: Avoidance and Defensive Behavior. During this phase recovering people don't want to think about anything that will cause the painful and uncomfortable feelings to come back. As a result they begin to avoid anything or anybody that will force an honest look at self. When asked direct questions about well-being, they tend to become defensive. The most common symptoms are:

☐ 3-1. *Believing "I'll Never Drink Again."* Recovering people often convince themselves that they will never drink or use again. Sometimes they tell this to others, but usually they keep it to themselves. They may be afraid to tell their counselor or other AA members about this belief. When they firmly believe they will never drink or use again, the need for a daily recovery program seems less important.

☐ 3-2. *Worrying About Others Instead of Self.* They may become more concerned about the sobriety of others than about personal recovery. They don't talk directly about these concerns but privately judge the drinking of friends and spouse and the recovery programs of other recovering persons. When dealing with issues of sobriety the recovering person begins to focus more on what other persons are doing rather than upon what he or she is doing. In AA this is called "working the other guy's program."

☐ 3-3. *Defensiveness.* They may have a tendency to defend themselves when talking about personal problems or their recovery program even when no defense is necessary.

☐ 3-4. *Compulsive Behavior.* They may become compulsive ("stuck" or "fixed" or "rigid") in the way they think and behave. There is a tendency to do the same things over and over again without a good reason. There is a tendency to control conversations either by talking too much or not talking at all. They tend to work more than is needed, become involved in many activities and may appear to be the model of recovery because of heavy involvement in AA Twelve Step work and chairing AA meetings. They may be leaders in counseling groups by "playing therapist." Casual or informal involvement with people, however, is avoided.

☐ 3-5. *Impulsive Behavior.* Patterns of compulsive behavior begin to be interrupted by impulsive reactions. In many cases these are over-reactions to stressful situations. High-stress situations that lasted for a long time generally resulted in impulsive behavior. Many times these overreactions to stress form the basis of decisions which affect major life areas and commitments to ongoing treatment.

☐ 3-6. **Tendencies Toward Loneliness.** They may begin to spend more time alone. They usually have good reasons and excuses for staying away from other people. These periods of being alone begin to occur more often and they begin to feel more and more lonely. Instead of dealing with the loneliness by trying to meet and be around other people, their behavior becomes more compulsive and impulsive.

Phase IV: Crisis Building. During this phase recovering people begin to experience a sequence of life problems that are caused by denying personal feelings, isolating self, and neglecting the recovery program. Even though they want to solve these problems and work hard at it, two new problems pop up to replace every problem that is solved. The most common warning signs that occur during this period are:

☐ 4-1. **Tunnel Vision.** Tunnel vision is seeing only one small part of life and not being able to get "the big picture." Many recovering people look at life as being made up of separate, unrelated parts. They focus on one part without looking at the other parts or how they are related. Sometimes this creates the mistaken belief that everything is secure and going well. At other times this results in seeing only what is going wrong. Small problems are blown up out of proportion. When this happens they come to believe they are being treated unfairly and have no power to do anything about it.

☐ 4-2. **Minor Depression.** Symptoms of depression begin to appear and to persist. They may feel down, blue, listless, empty of feelings. Oversleeping becomes common. They are able to distract themself from these moods by getting busy with other things and not talking about the depression.

☐ 4-3. **Loss of Constructive Planning.** They may stop planning each day and the future. They often mistake the AA slogan, "One day at a time," to mean that they shouldn't plan or think about what they are going to do. Less and less attention is paid to details. They become listless. Plans are based more on wishful thinking (how they wish things would be) than reality (how things actually are).

☐ 4-4. **Plans Begin to Fail.** Because they make plans that are not realistic and do not pay attention to details, plans begin to fail. Each failure causes new life problems. Some of these problems are similar to the problems that occurred during drinking. These typically include marital, work, social, and money problems. They often feel guilty and remorseful when these problems occur.

Phase V: Immobilization. During this phase the recovering person is unable to initiate action. He or she goes through the motions of living but is controlled by life rather than controlling life.

☐ 5-1. **Daydreaming and Wishful Thinking.** It becomes more difficult to concentrate. The "if only" syndrome becomes more common in conversation. They begin to have fantasies of escaping or "being rescued from it all" by an event unlikely to happen.

☐ 5-2. **Feelings That Nothing Can Be Solved.** A sense of failure begins to develop. The failure may be real or may be imagined. Small failures are exaggerated and blown out of proportion. The belief that "I've tried my best and recovery isn't working out" begins to develop.

☐ 5-3. **Immature Wish to Be Happy.** A vague desire "to be happy" or to have "things work out" may develop without their identifying what is necessary to be happy or have things work out. "Magical thinking is used." They want things to get better without doing anything to make them better, without paying the price of making things better.

Phase VI: Confusion and Overreaction. During this period recovering people have trouble thinking clearly. They become upset with themselves and those around them. They become irritable and overreact to small things. The most common warning signs experienced during this phase are:

☐ 6-1. **Periods of Confusion.** Periods of confusion become more frequent, last longer, and cause more problems. The recovering people experiencing this often feel angry with themselves because of their inability to figure things out.

☐ 6-2. **Irritation with Friends.** Relationships become strained with friends, family, counselors, and AA members. The recovering people may feel threatened when others talk about the changes they are noticing in their behavior and mood. The conflicts continue to increase in spite of their efforts to resolve them. They begin to feel guilty and remorseful about their role in these conflicts.

☐ 6-3. **Easily Angered.** They may experience episodes of anger, frustration, resentment, and irritability for no real reason. Overreaction to small things becomes more frequent. Stress and anxiety increase because of the fear that overreaction might result in violence. The effort to control themselves adds to the stress and tension.

Phase VII: Depression. During this period the recovering people become so depressed that they have difficulty keeping to normal routines. At times there may be thoughts of suicide, drinking, or drug use as a way to end the depression. The depression is severe and persistent and cannot be eaily ignored or hidden from others. The most common warning signs that occur during this period are:

☐ 7-1. **Irregular Eating Habits.** They may begin overeating or undereating. There is weight gain or loss. They stop having meals at regular times and replace a well-balanced, nourishing diet with "junk food."

☐ 7-2. **Lack of Desire to Take Action.** There may be periods when they are unable to get started or to get anything done. At those times they are unable to concentrate, feel anxious, fearful, and uneasy, and often feel trapped with no way out.

☐ 7-3. **Irregular Sleeping Habits.** They may have difficulty sleeping or be restless and fitful when they do sleep. Sleep is often marked by strange and frightening dreams. Because of exhaustion, they may sleep for 12 to 20 hours at a time. These "sleeping marathons" happen as often as every 6 to 15 days.

☐ 7-4. **Loss of Daily Structure:** Daily routine becomes haphazard. They stop getting up and going to bed at regular times. Sometimes they are unable to sleep, and this results in oversleeping at other times. Regular mealtimes are discontinued. It becomes more difficult to keep appointments and plan social events. They feel rushed and overburdened at times and then have nothing to do at other times. They are unable to follow through on plans and decisions and experience tension, frustration, fear, or anxiety that keep them from doing what should be done.

☐ 7-5. **Periods of Deep Depression.** They feel depressed more often. The depression becomes worse, lasts longer, and interferes with living. The depression is so bad that it is noticed by others and cannot be easily denied. The depression is most severe during unplanned or unstructured periods of time. Fatigue, hunger, and loneliness make the depression worse. When they feel depressed, they separate from other people, become irritable and angry with others, and often complain that nobody cares or understands what they are going through.

Phase VIII: Behavioral Loss of Control. During this phase they become unable to control or regulate personal behavior and daily schedule. There is still heavy denial and no full awareness of being out of control. Their life becomes chaotic and many problems are created in all areas of life and recovery. The most common warning signs experienced during this period are:

☐ 8-1. **Irregular Attendance at AA and Treatment Meetings.** They stop attending AA regularly and begin to miss scheduled appointments for counseling or treatment. They find excuses to justify this and do not recognize the importance of AA and treatment. They develop the attitude that "AA and counseling aren't making me feel better, so why should I make them a number one priority? Other things are more important."

☐ 8-2. **Development of an "I Don't Care" Attitude.** They try to act as if they don't care about the problems that are occurring. This is to hide feelings of helplessness and a growing lack of self-respect and self-confidence.

☐ 8-3. **Open Rejection of Help.** They cut

themself off from people who can help. They may do this by having fits of anger that drive others away, by criticizing and putting others down, or by quietly withdrawing from others.

☐ 8-4. **Dissatisfaction with Life.** Things seem so bad that they begin to think that they might as well begin addictive use because things couldn't get worse. Life seems to have become unmanageable since drinking has stopped.

☐ 8-5. **Feelings of Powerlessness and Helplessness.** They develop difficulty in "getting started"; have trouble thinking clearly, concentrating, and thinking abstractly; and feel that they can't do anything and begin to believe that there is no way out.

Phase IX: Recognition of Loss of Control. Their denial breaks and they suddenly recognize how severe the problems are, how unmanageable life has become, and how little power and control they have to solve any of the problems. This awareness is very painful and frightening. By this time they have become so isolated that it seems that there is no one to turn to for help. The most common warning signs that occur during this phase are:

☐ 9-1. **Self-Pity.** They begin to feel sorry for themselves and may use self-pity to get attention at AA or from family members.

☐ 9-2. **Thoughts of Social Drinking.** They realize that drinking or using drugs would help them to feel better and begin to hope that they can drink or use normally again and be able to control it. Sometimes they are able to put these thoughts out of their minds, but often the thoughts are so strong that they can't be stopped. They may begin to feel that drinking is the only alternative to going crazy or committing suicide. Drinking actually looks like a sane and rational alternative.

☐ 9-3. **Conscious Lying.** They begin to recognize the lying, denial, and excuses but are unable to interrupt them.

☐ 9-4. **Complete Loss of Self-Confidence.** They feel trapped and overwhelmed by the inability to think clearly and take action. This feeling of powerlessness causes the belief that they are useless and incompetent. As a result, they come

to believe that they can't manage life.

Phase X: Option Reduction. During this phase the recovering people feel trapped by the pain and inability to manage life. There seem to be only three ways out—insanity, suicide, or addictive use. They no longer believe that anyone or anything can help them. The most common warning signs that occur during this phase are:

☐ 10-1. **Unreasonable Resentment.** They feel angry because of the inability to behave the way they want to. Sometimes the anger is with the world in general, sometimes with someone or something in particular, and sometimes with self.

☐ 10-2. **Discontinues All Treatment and AA.** They stop attending all AA meetings. If they are taking Antabuse they may forget to take it or deliberately avoid taking it regularly. If a sponsor or helping person is part of treatment, tension and conflict develop and become so severe that the relationship usually ends. They may drop out of professional counseling even though they need help and know it.

☐ 10-3. **Overwhelming Loneliness, Frustration, Anger, and Tension.** They feel completely overwhelmed. They believe that there is no way out except drinking, suicide, or insanity. There are intense fears of insanity and feelings of helplessness and desperation.

☐ 10-4. **Loss of Behavioral Control.** They experience more and more difficulty in controlling thoughts, emotions, judgments, and behaviors. This progressive and disabling loss of control begins to cause serious problems in all areas of life. It begins to affect health. No matter how hard they try to regain control, they are unable to do so.

Phase XI: Return to Addictive Use or Physical/Emotional Collapse

☐ 11-1. **Return to "Controlled" Addictive Use.** At this point many recovering people are so desperate that they make themselves believe that controlled use is possible. They plan to use an addictive for a short period of time and/or in a controlled fashion. They begin using the addictive with the best of intentions. They believe they have no other choice.

☐ 11-2. *Shame and Guilt.* The initial use produces feelings of intense guilt and shame. Guilt is the feeling that is caused by the self-judgment that "I have done something wrong." The recently relapsed persons feel morally responsible for the return to use and believe it would not have happened if they had done "the right things." Shame is the feeling that results from the self-judgment that "I am a defective person." Many recovering people feel that their relapse proves that they are worthless and that they might as well die as an active addict.

☐ 11-3. *Loss of Control.* The addictive use spirals out of control. Sometimes that loss of control occurs slowly. At other times the loss of control is very rapid. The person begins using as often and as much as before.

☐ 11-4. *Life and Health Problems.* They begin to experience severe problems with their life and health. Marriage, jobs, and friendships are seriously damaged. Eventually their physical health suffers and they become so ill that they need professional treatment.

The Staying Sober Workbook by Terence T. Gorski
Available from: Independence Press, P.O. Box HH, Independence, MO 64055

Name: _____

THE INITIAL WARNING SIGN LIST

INSTRUCTIONS: Select the five warning signs that are most important to you. Read each one and underline a word or phrase that best summarizes its meaning. Copy the summary title and underlined word and answer the final questions.

The First Most Important Warning Sign

1. Summary Title: _____.

2. Underlined Word: _____.

3. Why is this warning sign important to you? _____

_____.

4. Please describe this personal warning sign of relapse beginning with the words: "I KNOW MY RECOVERY IS IN TROUBLE WHEN..."

_____.

_____.

The Second Most Important Warning Sign

5. Summary Title: _____.

6. Underlined Word: _____.

7. Why is this warning sign important to you? _____

_____.

8. Please describe this personal warning sign of relapse beginning with the words: "I KNOW MY RECOVERY IS IN TROUBLE WHEN..."

_____.

_____.

The Third Most Important Warning Sign

9. Summary Title: _____.

10. Underlined Word: _____.

11. Why is this warning sign important to you? _____

_____.

12. Please describe this personal warning sign of relapse beginning with the words: "I KNOW MY RECOVERY IS IN TROUBLE WHEN..."

_____.

_____.

The Fourth Most Important Warning Sign

13. Summary Title: _____.

14. Underlined Word: _____.

15. Why is this warning sign important to you? _____
_____.

16. Please describe this personal warning sign of relapse beginning with the words: "I KNOW MY RECOVERY IS IN TROUBLE WHEN..."

_____.

_____.

The Fifth Most Important Warning Sign

17. Summary Title: _____.

18. Underlined Word: _____.

19. Why is this warning sign important to you? _____
_____.

20. Please describe this personal warning sign of relapse beginning with the words: "I KNOW MY RECOVERY IS IN TROUBLE WHEN..."

_____.

_____.

Once you have completed the process for the five warning signs that you selected, answer the following:

21. Please describe what you were thinking when you were completing this worksheet.

_____.

_____.

_____.

_____.

_____.

22. Please describe how you were feeling when you were completing this worksheet.

_____.

_____.

_____.

_____.

_____.

23. Please complete the following sentence as rapidly as you can with ten different endings: "I am now becoming aware that..."

1. _____ .

2. _____ .

3. _____ .

4. _____ .

5. _____ .

6. _____ .

7. _____ .

8. _____ .

9. _____ .

10. _____ .

24. Often there is a similarity or a relationship between some of the warning signs that you have selected. You may or may not see those patterns at this time. If you do, please describe any patterns or recurring themes in the warning signs that you selected.

_____

_____ .

_____ .

_____ .

_____ .

_____ .

25. Identify any stuck points or unresolved issues in your recovery that you are aware of that must be dealt with in order to prevent these warning signs from coming back in the future.

_____ .

_____ .

_____ .

_____ .

_____ .

_____ .

_____ .

_____ .

The Staying Sober Workbook by Terence T. Gorski
Available from: Independence Press, P.O. Box HH, Independence, MO 64055

WARNING SIGN ANALYSIS

Complete this exercise using your most important warning sign. There are five worksheets just like this one. The others will be used for your other four warning signs. You will need to read the complete instructions for this exercise found on pages 30–40 of the instruction manual. Open the instruction manual to those pages while you complete this exercise. When you have completed worksheet #1 go on to worksheet #2.

PRIORITY WARNING SIGN #1 (Your most important warning sign.)

1. **Summary Title:** _____.

2. **Underlined Word:** _____.

3. **Personal Summary Title:** Rewrite the summary title in your own words:

   _____.

4. **Personal Description:** Please describe what you think and how you feel and act when you are experiencing the warning sign.

   _____.

   _____.

   _____.

   _____.

   _____.

5. **Main Ideas:**

   1. _____.

   2. _____.

   3. _____.

   4. _____.

   5. _____.

6. **Past Experience:** Please describe a past experience with the warning sign:

   _____.

   _____.

   _____.

   _____.

   _____.

7. **Main Ideas:**

    1. _____ .

    2. _____ .

    3. _____ .

    4. _____ .

    5. _____ .

8. **Future Experience:** Please describe how you think this warning sign may happen in the future:

_____ .

_____ .

9. **Main Ideas:**

    1. _____ .

    2. _____ .

    3. _____ .

    4. _____ .

    5. _____ .

10. **Combined List:** Please make a combined list of the main ideas that you have related to this warning sign. Try to eliminate duplicate or similar items.

    1. _____ .

    2. _____ .

    3. _____ .

    4. _____ .

    5. _____ .

    6. _____ .

    7. _____ .

    8. _____ .

    9. _____ .

    10. _____ .

    11. _____ .

    12. _____ .

    13. _____ .

    14. _____ .

    15. _____ .

11. **Sequence of Events:** There is a sequence of events that leads to this warning sign. Please write out this sequence of events.

☐ Event 1: Summary Title:_____

Description: _____

_____

_____

☐ Event 2: Summary Title:_____

Description: _____

_____

_____

☐ Event 3: Summary Title:_____

Description: _____

_____

_____

☐ Event 4: Summary Title:_____

Description: _____

_____

_____

☐ Event 5: Summary Title:_____

Description: _____

_____

_____

☐ Event 6: Summary Title:_____

Description: _____

_____

_____

☐ Event 7: Summary Title:_____

Description: _____

_____

_____

☐ Event 8: Summary Title:_____

Description: _____

_____

☐ Event 9: Summary Title:_____

Description: _____

_____

☐ Event 10: Summary Title:_____

Description: _____

_____

☐ Event 11: Summary Title:_____

Description: _____

_____

☐ Event 12: Summary Title:_____

Description: _____

_____

☐ Event 13: Summary Title:_____

Description: _____

_____

☐ Event 14: Summary Title:_____

Description: _____

_____

☐ Event 15: Summary Title:_____

Description: _____

_____

Now go back and put a check in front of any event that can be a warning sign in its own right. Actually these events are earlier warning signs that, if identified and interrupted, can prevent your priority warning sign from occurring.

The Staying Sober Workbook by Terence T. Gorski
Available from: Independence Press, P.O. Box HH, Independence, MO 64055

Exercise 13
(worksheet #2)

WARNING SIGN ANALYSIS

Complete this exercise using your second most important warning sign. This is the second of five worksheets for Exercise 13. You will need to open pages 30–40 of your instruction manual while you complete all of these worksheets. When you have completed worksheet #2 go on to worksheet #3.

PRIORITY WARNING SIGN #1 (Your most important warning sign.)

1. **Summary Title:** _____.

2. **Underlined Word:** _____.

3. **Personal Summary Title:** Rewrite the summary title in your own words:

   _____.

4. **Personal Description:** Please describe what you think and how you feel and act when you are experiencing the warning sign.

   _____.

   _____.

   _____.

   _____.

   _____.

5. **Main Ideas:**

   1. _____.

   2. _____.

   3. _____.

   4. _____.

   5. _____.

6. **Past Experience:** Please describe a past experience with the warning sign:

   _____.

   _____.

   _____.

   _____.

7. **Main Ideas:**

1. _____.
2. _____.
3. _____.
4. _____.
5. _____.

8. **Future Experience:** Please describe how you think this warning sign may happen in the future:

_____.
_____.
_____.

9. **Main Ideas:**

1. _____.
2. _____.
3. _____.
4. _____.
5. _____.

10. **Combined List:** Please make a combined list of the main ideas that you have related to this warning sign. Try to eliminate duplicate or similar items.

1. _____.
2. _____.
3. _____.
4. _____.
5. _____.
6. _____.
7. _____.
8. _____.
9. _____.
10. _____.
11. _____.
12. _____.
13. _____.
14. _____.
15. _____.

11. **Sequence of Events:** There is a sequence of events that leads to this warning sign. Please write out this sequence of events.

☐ Event 1: Summary Title:_____

Description: _____

_____

_____

☐ Event 2: Summary Title:_____

Description: _____

_____

_____

☐ Event 3: Summary Title:_____

Description: _____

_____

_____

☐ Event 4: Summary Title:_____

Description: _____

_____

_____

☐ Event 5: Summary Title:_____

Description: _____

_____

_____

☐ Event 6: Summary Title:_____

Description: _____

_____

_____

☐ Event 7: Summary Title:_____

Description: _____

_____

_____

☐ Event 8: Summary Title:_____

Description: _____

_____

☐ Event 9: Summary Title:_____

Description: _____

_____

☐ Event 10: Summary Title: _____

Description: _____

_____

☐ Event 11: Summary Title: _____

Description: _____

_____

☐ Event 12: Summary Title: _____

Description: _____

_____

☐ Event 13: Summary Title: _____

Description: _____

_____

☐ Event 14: Summary Title: _____

Description: _____

_____

☐ Event 15: Summary Title: _____

Description: _____

_____

Now go back and put a check in front of any event that can be a warning sign in its own right. Actually these events are earlier warning signs that, if identified and interrupted, can prevent your priority warning sign from occurring.

The Staying Sober Workbook by Terence T. Gorski
Available from: Independence Press, P.O. Box HH, Independence, MO 64055

WARNING SIGN ANALYSIS

Complete this exercise using your third most important warning sign. This is the third of five worksheets for Exercise 13. You will need to open pages 30–40 of your instruction manual while you complete all of these worksheets. When you have completed worksheet #3 go on to worksheet #4.

PRIORITY WARNING SIGN #1 (Your most important warning sign.)

1. **Summary Title:** _____.

2. **Underlined Word:** _____.

3. **Personal Summary Title:** Rewrite the summary title in your own words:

    _____.

4. **Personal Description:** Please describe what you think and how you feel and act when you are experiencing the warning sign.

    _____.

    _____.

    _____.

    _____.

    _____.

5. **Main Ideas:**

    1. _____.

    2. _____.

    3. _____.

    4. _____.

    5. _____.

6. **Past Experience:** Please describe a past experience with the warning sign:

    _____.

    _____.

    _____.

    _____.

    _____.

7. **Main Ideas:**

1. _____.
2. _____.
3. _____.
4. _____.
5. _____.

8. **Future Experience:** Please describe how you think this warning sign may happen in the future:

_____.

_____.

_____.

9. **Main Ideas:**

1. _____.
2. _____.
3. _____.
4. _____.
5. _____.

10. **Combined List:** Please make a combined list of the main ideas that you have related to this warning sign. Try to eliminate duplicate or similar items.

1. _____.
2. _____.
3. _____.
4. _____.
5. _____.
6. _____.
7. _____.
8. _____.
9. _____.
10. _____.
11. _____.
12. _____.
13. _____.
14. _____.
15. _____.

11. **Sequence of Events:** There is a sequence of events that leads to this warning sign. Please write out this sequence of events.

☐ Event 1: Summary Title:_____

Description: _____

_____

_____

☐ Event 2: Summary Title:_____

Description: _____

_____

_____

☐ Event 3: Summary Title:_____

Description: _____

_____

_____

☐ Event 4: Summary Title:_____

Description: _____

_____

_____

☐ Event 5: Summary Title:_____

Description: _____

_____

_____

☐ Event 6: Summary Title:_____

Description: _____

_____

_____

☐ Event 7: Summary Title:_____

Description: _____

_____

_____

☐ Event 8: Summary Title:_____

Description: _____

_____

☐ Event 9: Summary Title:_____

Description: _____

_____

☐ Event 10: Summary Title: _____

Description: _____

_____

☐ Event 11: Summary Title: _____

Description: _____

_____

☐ Event 12: Summary Title: _____

Description: _____

_____

☐ Event 13: Summary Title: _____

Description: _____

_____

☐ Event 14: Summary Title: _____

Description: _____

_____

☐ Event 15: Summary Title: _____

Description: _____

_____

Now go back and put a check in front of any event that can be a warning sign in its own right. Actually these events are earlier warning signs that, if identified and interrupted, can prevent your priority warning sign from occurring.

The Staying Sober Workbook by Terence T. Gorski
Available from: Independence Press, P.O. Box HH, Independence, MO 64055

Name: _____

WARNING SIGN ANALYSIS

Complete this exercise using your fourth most important warning sign. This is the fourth of five worksheets for Exercise 13. You will need to open pages 30–40 of your instruction manual while you complete all of these worksheets. When you have completed worksheet #4 go on to worksheet #5.

PRIORITY WARNING SIGN #1 (Your most important warning sign.)

1. **Summary Title:** _____.

2. **Underlined Word:** _____.

3. **Personal Summary Title:** Rewrite the summary title in your own words:

   _____.

4. **Personal Description:** Please describe what you think and how you feel and act when you are experiencing the warning sign.

   _____.

   _____.

   _____.

   _____.

   _____.

5. **Main Ideas:**

   1. _____.

   2. _____.

   3. _____.

   4. _____.

   5. _____.

6. **Past Experience:** Please describe a past experience with the warning sign:

   _____.

   _____.

   _____.

   _____.

   _____.

7. **Main Ideas:**

1. _____.

2. _____.

3. _____.

4. _____.

5. _____.

8. **Future Experience:** Please describe how you think this warning sign may happen in the future:

_____.

_____.

_____.

9. **Main Ideas:**

1. _____.

2. _____.

3. _____.

4. _____.

5. _____.

10. **Combined List:** Please make a combined list of the main ideas that you have related to this warning sign. Try to eliminate duplicate or similar items.

1. _____.

2. _____.

3. _____.

4. _____.

5. _____.

6. _____.

7. _____.

8. _____.

9. _____.

10. _____.

11. _____.

12. _____.

13. _____.

14. _____.

15. _____.

11. **Sequence of Events:** There is a sequence of events that leads to this warning sign. Please write out this sequence of events.

☐ Event 1: Summary Title:_____

Description: _____

_____

_____

☐ Event 2: Summary Title:_____

Description: _____

_____

_____

☐ Event 3: Summary Title:_____

Description: _____

_____

_____

☐ Event 4: Summary Title:_____

Description: _____

_____

_____

☐ Event 5: Summary Title:_____

Description: _____

_____

_____

☐ Event 6: Summary Title:_____

Description: _____

_____

_____

☐ Event 7: Summary Title:_____

Description: _____

_____

_____

☐ Event 8: Summary Title:_____

Description: _____

_____

☐ Event 9: Summary Title:_____

Description: _____

_____

☐ Event 10: Summary Title: _____

Description: _____

_____

☐ Event 11: Summary Title: _____

Description: _____

_____

☐ Event 12: Summary Title: _____

Description: _____

_____

☐ Event 13: Summary Title: _____

Description: _____

_____

☐ Event 14: Summary Title: _____

Description: _____

_____

☐ Event 15: Summary Title: _____

Description: _____

_____

Now go back and put a check in front of any event that can be a warning sign in its own right. Actually these events are earlier warning signs that, if identified and interrupted, can prevent your priority warning sign from occurring.

The Staying Sober Workbook by Terence T. Gorski
Available from: Independence Press, P.O. Box HH, Independence, MO 64055

Name: _____

WARNING SIGN ANALYSIS

Complete this exercise using your fifth most important warning sign. This is the last of five worksheets for Exercise 13. You will need to open pages 30–40 of your instruction manual while you complete all of these worksheets. When you have completed worksheet #5, review all of them in preparation for Exercise 14: Warning Sign Grouping.

PRIORITY WARNING SIGN #1 (Your most important warning sign.)

1. **Summary Title:** _____.

2. **Underlined Word:** _____.

3. **Personal Summary Title:** Rewrite the summary title in your own words:

   _____.

4. **Personal Description:** Please describe what you think and how you feel and act when you are experiencing the warning sign.

   _____.

   _____.

   _____.

   _____.

   _____.

5. **Main Ideas:**

   1. _____.

   2. _____.

   3. _____.

   4. _____.

   5. _____.

6. **Past Experience:** Please describe a past experience with the warning sign:

   _____.

   _____.

   _____.

   _____.

   _____.

7. **Main Ideas:**

    1. _____.

    2. _____.

    3. _____.

    4. _____.

    5. _____.

8. **Future Experience:** Please describe how you think this warning sign may happen in the future:

_____.

_____.

_____.

9. **Main Ideas:**

    1. _____.

    2. _____.

    3. _____.

    4. _____.

    5. _____.

10. **Combined List:** Please make a combined list of the main ideas that you have related to this warning sign. Try to eliminate duplicate or similar items.

    1. _____.

    2. _____.

    3. _____.

    4. _____.

    5. _____.

    6. _____.

    7. _____.

    8. _____.

    9. _____.

    10. _____.

    11. _____.

    12. _____.

    13. _____.

    14. _____.

    15. _____.

11. **Sequence of Events:** There is a sequence of events that leads to this warning sign. Please write out this sequence of events.

☐ Event 1: Summary Title:_____

Description: _____

_____

_____

☐ Event 2: Summary Title:_____

Description: _____

_____

_____

☐ Event 3: Summary Title:_____

Description: _____

_____

_____

☐ Event 4: Summary Title:_____

Description: _____

_____

_____

☐ Event 5: Summary Title:_____

Description: _____

_____

_____

☐ Event 6: Summary Title:_____

Description: _____

_____

_____

☐ Event 7: Summary Title:_____

Description: _____

_____

_____

☐ Event 8: Summary Title:_____

Description: _____

_____

☐ Event 9: Summary Title:_____

Description: _____

_____

☐ Event 10: Summary Title: _____

Description: _____

_____

☐ Event 11: Summary Title: _____

Description: _____

_____

☐ Event 12: Summary Title: _____

Description: _____

_____

☐ Event 13: Summary Title: _____

Description: _____

_____

☐ Event 14: Summary Title: _____

Description: _____

_____

☐ Event 15: Summary Title: _____

Description: _____

_____

Now go back and put a check in front of any event that can be a warning sign in its own right. Actually these events are earlier warning signs that, if identified and interrupted, can prevent your priority warning sign from occurring.

The Staying Sober Workbook by Terence T. Gorski
Available from: Independence Press, P.O. Box HH, Independence, MO 64055

Name: _____

RELAPSE WARNING SIGN GROUPING

Part 1: Review the Sequence of Events (Item 11) on all five worksheets of Exercise 13: Warning Sign Analysis. Select a category that will be useful in grouping similar warning signs and describe that category below.

Group #1: Warning signs that refer to _____.

_____

List the number and the summary title of all items listed in the Sequence of Events that belong to the above category.

#_____: Summary Title: _____.

#_____: Summary Title: _____.

#_____: Summary Title: _____.

#_____: Summary Title: _____.

#_____: Summary Title: _____.

Part 2: Write new warning signs that will include the key ideas listed above while eliminating duplication.

#_____: Summary Title: _____.

Description: _____

_____

_____

_____

#_____: Summary Title: _____.

Description: _____

_____

_____

_____

#_____: Summary Title: _____.

Description: _____

_____

_____

_____

The Staying Sober Workbook by Terence T. Gorski
Available from: Independence Press, P.O. Box HH, Independence, MO 64055

RELAPSE WARNING SIGN GROUPING

Part 1: Review the Sequence of Events (Item 11) on all five worksheets of Exercise 13: Warning Sign Analysis. Select a category that will be useful in grouping similar warning signs and describe that category below.

Group #2: Warning signs that refer to _____

_____

List the number and the summary title of all items listed in the Sequence of Events that belong to the above category.

#_____: Summary Title: _____.

#_____: Summary Title: _____.

#_____: Summary Title: _____.

#_____: Summary Title: _____.

#_____: Summary Title: _____.

Part 2: Write new warning signs that will include the key ideas listed above while eliminating duplication.

#_____: Summary Title: _____.

Description: _____

_____

_____

_____.

#_____: Summary Title: _____.

Description: _____

_____

_____

_____.

#_____: Summary Title: _____.

Description: _____

_____

_____

_____.

The Staying Sober Workbook by Terence T. Gorski
Available from: Independence Press, P.O. Box HH, Independence, MO 64055

Name: _____

RELAPSE WARNING SIGN GROUPING

Part 1: Review the Sequence of Events (Item 11) on all five worksheets of Exercise 13: Warning Sign Analysis. Select a category that will be useful in grouping similar warning signs and describe that category below.

Group #3: Warning signs that refer to _____

_____

List the number and the summary title of all items listed in the Sequence of Events that belong to the above category.

#_____: Summary Title: _____.

#_____: Summary Title: _____.

#_____: Summary Title: _____.

#_____: Summary Title: _____.

#_____: Summary Title: _____.

Part 2: Write new warning signs that will include the key ideas listed above while eliminating duplication.

#_____: Summary Title: _____.

Description: _____

_____

_____

_____

#_____: Summary Title: _____.

Description: _____

_____

_____

_____

#_____: Summary Title: _____.

Description: _____

_____

_____

_____

The Staying Sober Workbook by Terence T. Gorski
Available from: Independence Press, P.O. Box HH, Independence, MO 64055

RELAPSE WARNING SIGN GROUPING

Part 1: Review the Sequence of Events (Item 11) on all five worksheets of Exercise 13: Warning Sign Analysis. Select a category that will be useful in grouping similar warning signs and describe that category below.

Group #4: Warning signs that refer to _____

_____

List the number and the summary title of all items listed in the Sequence of Events that belong to the above category.

#_____: Summary Title: _____.

#_____: Summary Title: _____.

#_____: Summary Title: _____.

#_____: Summary Title: _____.

#_____: Summary Title: _____.

Part 2: Write new warning signs that will include the key ideas listed above while eliminating duplication.

#_____: Summary Title: _____.

Description: _____

_____

_____

_____.

#_____: Summary Title: _____.

Description: _____

_____

_____

_____.

#_____: Summary Title: _____.

Description: _____

_____

_____

_____.

The Staying Sober Workbook by Terence T. Gorski
Available from: Independence Press, P.O. Box HH, Independence, MO 64055

Name: _____

RELAPSE WARNING SIGN GROUPING

Part 1: Review the Sequence of Events (Item 11) on all five worksheets of Exercise 13: Warning Sign Analysis. Select a category that will be useful in grouping similar warning signs and describe that category below.

Group #5: Warning signs that refer to _____

_____

List the number and the summary title of all items listed in the Sequence of Events that belong to the above category.

#_____: Summary Title: _____.

#_____: Summary Title: _____.

#_____: Summary Title: _____.

#_____: Summary Title: _____.

#_____: Summary Title: _____.

Part 2: Write new warning signs that will include the key ideas listed above while eliminating duplication.

#_____: Summary Title: _____.

Description: _____

_____

_____

_____.

#_____: Summary Title: _____.

Description: _____

_____

_____

_____.

#_____: Summary Title: _____.

Description: _____

_____

_____

_____.

RELAPSE WARNING SIGN GROUPING

Part 1: Review the Sequence of Events (Item 11) on all five worksheets of Exercise 13: Warning Sign Analysis. Select a category that will be useful in grouping similar warning signs and describe that category below.

Group #6: Warning signs that refer to _____

_____

List the number and the summary title of all items listed in the Sequence of Events that belong to the above category.

#_____: Summary Title: _____.

#_____: Summary Title: _____.

#_____: Summary Title: _____.

#_____: Summary Title: _____.

#_____: Summary Title: _____.

Part 2: Write new warning signs that will include the key ideas listed above while eliminating duplication.

#_____: Summary Title: _____.

Description: _____

_____

_____

_____.

#_____: Summary Title: _____.

Description: _____

_____

_____

_____.

#_____: Summary Title: _____.

Description: _____

_____

_____

_____.

Name: _____

RELAPSE WARNING SIGN GROUPING

Part 1: Review the Sequence of Events (Item 11) on all five worksheets of Exercise 13: Warning Sign Analysis. Select a category that will be useful in grouping similar warning signs and describe that category below.

Group #7: Warning signs that refer to _____

_____

List the number and the summary title of all items listed in the Sequence of Events that belong to the above category.

#_____: Summary Title: _____.

#_____: Summary Title: _____.

#_____: Summary Title: _____.

#_____: Summary Title: _____.

#_____: Summary Title: _____.

Part 2: Write new warning signs that will include the key ideas listed above while eliminating duplication.

#_____: Summary Title: _____.

Description: _____

_____

_____

_____

#_____: Summary Title: _____.

Description: _____

_____

_____

_____

#_____: Summary Title: _____.

Description: _____

_____

_____

_____

RELAPSE WARNING SIGN GROUPING

Part 1: Review the Sequence of Events (Item 11) on all five worksheets of Exercise 13: Warning Sign Analysis. Select a category that will be useful in grouping similar warning signs and describe that category below.

Group #8: Warning signs that refer to _____

_____

List the number and the summary title of all items listed in the Sequence of Events that belong to the above category.

#_____: Summary Title: _____.

#_____: Summary Title: _____.

#_____: Summary Title: _____.

#_____: Summary Title: _____.

#_____: Summary Title: _____.

Part 2: Write new warning signs that will include the key ideas listed above while eliminating duplication.

#_____: Summary Title: _____.

Description: _____

_____

_____

_____.

#_____: Summary Title: _____.

Description: _____

_____

_____

_____.

#_____: Summary Title: _____.

Description: _____

_____

_____

_____.

Exercise 15   **Name:** _____

THE FINAL WARNING SIGN LIST

==

PERSONAL WARNING SIGN #1:

1–1.   Summary Title: _____

1–2.   Description: I know I am in trouble with my recovery when:

_____

_____

_____

_____ .

1–4.   When this happens I tend to think: _____

_____ .

1–3.   When this happens I tend to feel: _____

_____ .

1–5.   When this happens I want to: _____

_____ .

==

PERSONAL WARNING SIGN #2:

2–1.   Summary Title: _____

2–2.   Description: I know I am in trouble with my recovery when:

_____

_____

_____

_____ .

2–4.   When this happens I tend to think: _____

_____ .

2–3.   When this happens I tend to feel: _____

_____ .

2–5.   When this happens I want to: _____

_____ .

PERSONAL WARNING SIGN #3:

3–1. Summary Title: _____

3–2. Description: I know I am in trouble with my recovery when:

_____

_____

_____

_____

_____

_____.

3–4. When this happens I tend to think: _____

_____.

3–3. When this happens I tend to feel: _____

_____.

3–5. When this happens I want to: _____

_____

PERSONAL WARNING SIGN #4:

4–1. Summary Title: _____

4–2. Description: I know I am in trouble with my recovery when:

_____

_____

_____

_____

_____.

4–4. When this happens I tend to think: _____

_____

4–3. When this happens I tend to feel: _____

_____.

4–5. When this happens I want to: _____

_____

PERSONAL WARNING SIGN #5:

5–1.   Summary Title: _____

5–2.   Description: I know I am in trouble with my recovery when:

_____

_____

_____

_____

_____.

5–4.   When this happens I tend to think: _____

_____.

5–3.   When this happens I tend to feel: _____

_____.

5–5.   When this happens I want to: _____

_____.

PERSONAL WARNING SIGN #6:

6–1.   Summary Title: _____

6–2.   Description: I know I am in trouble with my recovery when:

_____

_____

_____

_____

_____.

6–4.   When this happens I tend to think: _____

_____.

6–3.   When this happens I tend to feel: _____

_____.

6–5.   When this happens I want to: _____

_____.

PERSONAL WARNING SIGN #7:

7-1.   Summary Title: _____

7-2.   Description: I know I am in trouble with my recovery when:

_____

_____

_____

_____

_____

_____.

7-4.   When this happens I tend to think: _____

_____.

7-3.   When this happens I tend to feel: _____

_____.

7-5.   When this happens I want to: _____

_____

PERSONAL WARNING SIGN #8:

8-1.   Summary Title: _____

8-2.   Description: I know I am in trouble with my recovery when:

_____

_____

_____

_____

_____.

8-4.   When this happens I tend to think: _____

_____

8-3.   When this happens I tend to feel: _____

_____.

8-5.   When this happens I want to: _____

_____

PERSONAL WARNING SIGN #9:

9–1.   Summary Title: _____

9–2.   Description: I know I am in trouble with my recovery when:

_____

_____

_____

_____

_____.

9–4.   When this happens I tend to think: _____

_____.

9–3.   When this happens I tend to feel: _____

_____.

9–5.   When this happens I want to: _____

_____.

PERSONAL WARNING SIGN #10:

10–1.   Summary Title:_____

10–2.   Description: I know I am in trouble with my recovery when:

_____

_____

_____

_____

_____.

10–4.   When this happens I tend to think: _____

_____.

10–3.   When this happens I tend to feel: _____

_____.

10–5.   When this happens I want to: _____

_____.

PERSONAL WARNING SIGN #11:

11–1.   Summary Title:_____

11–2.   Description: I know I am in trouble with my recovery when:

_____

_____

_____

_____

_____

_____ .

11–4.   When this happens I tend to think: _____

_____ .

11–3.   When this happens I tend to feel: _____

_____ .

11–5.   When this happens I want to: _____

_____

PERSONAL WARNING SIGN #12:

12–1.   Summary Title:_____

12–2.   Description: I know I am in trouble with my recovery when:

_____

_____

_____

_____

_____ .

12–4.   When this happens I tend to think: _____

_____

12–3.   When this happens I tend to feel: _____

_____ .

12–5.   When this happens I want to: _____

_____

PERSONAL WARNING SIGN #13:

13–1. Summary Title:_____

13–2. Description: I know I am in trouble with my recovery when:

_____

_____

_____

_____

_____ .

13–4. When this happens I tend to think: _____

_____ .

13–3. When this happens I tend to feel: _____

_____ .

13–5. When this happens I want to: _____

_____ .

PERSONAL WARNING SIGN #14:

14–1. Summary Title:_____

14–2. Description: I know I am in trouble with my recovery when:

_____

_____

_____

_____

_____ .

14–4. When this happens I tend to think:_____

_____ .

14–3. When this happens I tend to feel: _____

_____ .

14–5. When this happens I want to: _____

_____

PERSONAL WARNING SIGN #15:

15–1.   Summary Title:_____

15–2.   Description: I know I am in trouble with my recovery when:

_____

_____

_____

_____.

15–4.   When this happens I tend to think: _____

_____

15–3.   When this happens I tend to feel: _____

_____.

15–5.   When this happens I want to: _____

_____

The Staying Sober Workbook by Terence T. Gorski
Available from: Independence Press, P.O. Box HH, Independence, MO 64055;

WARNING SIGN MANAGEMENT

1. *Summary Title:* What is the warning sign you are learning to manage?

   _____

2. *Past Experience of Ineffective Management:* Please describe a past experience with this warning sign during which you were sober and managed it ineffectively.

   _____

   _____

   _____

   _____

   _____

3. *New Management Strategy:* If you had to experience this same situation again, what would you do differently to manage the warning sign more effectively?

   _____

   _____

   _____

   _____

   _____

4. What were the constructive thoughts that helped you manage this warning sign effectively?

   _____

   _____

   _____

   _____

   _____

5. What were the self-defeating thoughts that caused you to manage this warning sign ineffectively?

   _____

   _____

   _____

   _____

   _____

6. What did you feel when you imagined yourself managing the warning sign effectively?

   _____

   _____

   _____

   _____

   _____

7. What did you feel when you managed this warning sign ineffectively?

   _____

   _____

   _____

   _____

   _____

8. What were the constructive behaviors that helped you to manage this warning sign effectively?

_____

_____

_____

_____

_____

9. What were the self-defeating behaviors that caused you to manage this warning sign ineffectively?

_____

_____

_____

_____

_____

10. *Action Plan:* Please describe an action plan that could be used to successfully manage this warning sign in the future. (Be sure to include strategies for constructive thinking, emotional management, behavior change, and situational management.)

_____

_____

_____

_____

_____

_____

11. *Skills Needed:* What skills will you need to develop to be able to implement the action you described above?

_____

_____

_____

_____

_____

_____

_____

_____

_____

The Staying Sober Workbook by Terence T. Gorski
Available from: Independence Press, P.O. Box HH, Independence, MO 64055

Exercise 16
(worksheet _____)

Name: _____

WARNING SIGN MANAGEMENT

1. **Summary Title:** What is the warning sign you are learning to manage?

_____

2. **Past Experience of Ineffective Management:** Please describe a past experience with this warning sign during which you were sober and managed it ineffectively.

_____

_____

_____

_____

_____

3. **New Management Strategy:** If you had to experience this same situation again, what would you do differently to manage the warning sign more effectively?

_____

_____

_____

_____

_____

4. What were the constructive thoughts that helped you manage this warning sign effectively?

_____

_____

_____

_____

5. What were the self-defeating thoughts that caused you to manage this warning sign ineffectively?

_____

_____

_____

_____

6. What did you feel when you imagined yourself managing the warning sign effectively?

_____

_____

_____

_____

7. What did you feel when you managed this warning sign ineffectively?

_____

_____

_____

_____

8. What were the constructive behaviors that helped you to manage this warning sign effectively?

_____

_____

_____

_____

_____

_____

9. What were the self-defeating behaviors that caused you to manage this warning sign ineffectively?

_____

_____

_____

_____

_____

_____

10. *Action Plan:* Please describe an action plan that could be used to successfully manage this warning sign in the future. (Be sure to include strategies for constructive thinking, emotional management, behavior change, and situational management.)

_____

_____

_____

_____

_____

_____

_____

11. *Skills Needed:* What skills will you need to develop to be able to implement the action you described above?

_____

_____

_____

_____

_____

_____

_____

_____

_____

_____

_____

_____

The Staying Sober Workbook by Terence T. Gorski
Available from: Independence Press, P.O. Box HH, Independence, MO 64055;

WARNING SIGN MANAGEMENT

1. **Summary Title:** What is the warning sign you are learning to manage?

   _____

2. **Past Experience of Ineffective Management:** Please describe a past experience with this warning sign during which you were sober and managed it ineffectively.

   _____

   _____

   _____

   _____

   _____

3. **New Management Strategy:** If you had to experience this same situation again, what would you do differently to manage the warning sign more effectively?

   _____

   _____

   _____

   _____

   _____

4. What were the constructive thoughts that helped you manage this warning sign effectively?

   _____

   _____

   _____

   _____

   _____

5. What were the self-defeating thoughts that caused you to manage this warning sign ineffectively?

   _____

   _____

   _____

   _____

   _____

6. What did you feel when you imagined yourself managing the warning sign effectively?

   _____

   _____

   _____

   _____

   _____

7. What did you feel when you managed this warning sign ineffectively?

   _____

   _____

   _____

   _____

   _____

8. What were the constructive behaviors that helped you to manage this warning sign effectively?

_____

_____

_____

_____

_____

_____

9. What were the self-defeating behaviors that caused you to manage this warning sign ineffectively?

_____

_____

_____

_____

_____

_____

10. *Action Plan:* Please describe an action plan that could be used to successfully manage this warning sign in the future. (Be sure to include strategies for constructive thinking, emotional management, behavior change, and situational management.)

_____

_____

_____

_____

_____

_____

11. *Skills Needed:* What skills will you need to develop to be able to implement the action you described above?

_____

_____

_____

_____

_____

_____

_____

_____

_____

_____

The Staying Sober Workbook by Terence T. Gorski
Available from: Independence Press, P.O. Box HH, Independence, MO 64055

Name: _____

WARNING SIGN MANAGEMENT

1. *Summary Title:* What is the warning sign you are learning to manage?

   _____

2. *Past Experience of Ineffective Management:* Please describe a past experience with this warning sign during which you were sober and managed it ineffectively.

   _____

   _____

   _____

   _____

   _____

3. *New Management Strategy:* If you had to experience this same situation again, what would you do differently to manage the warning sign more effectively?

   _____

   _____

   _____

   _____

   _____

4. What were the constructive thoughts that helped you manage this warning sign effectively?

   _____

   _____

   _____

   _____

   _____

5. What were the self-defeating thoughts that caused you to manage this warning sign ineffectively?

   _____

   _____

   _____

   _____

   _____

6. What did you feel when you imagined yourself managing the warning sign effectively?

   _____

   _____

   _____

   _____

   _____

7. What did you feel when you managed this warning sign ineffectively?

   _____

   _____

   _____

   _____

   _____

8. What were the constructive behaviors that helped you to manage this warning sign effectively?

_____

_____

_____

_____

_____

9. What were the self-defeating behaviors that caused you to manage this warning sign ineffectively?

_____

_____

_____

_____

_____

10. *Action Plan:* Please describe an action plan that could be used to successfully manage this warning sign in the future. (Be sure to include strategies for constructive thinking, emotional management, behavior change, and situational management.)

_____

_____

_____

_____

_____

_____

11. *Skills Needed:* What skills will you need to develop to be able to implement the action you described above?

_____

_____

_____

_____

_____

_____

_____

_____

_____

_____

The Staying Sober Workbook by Terence T. Gorski
Available from: Independence Press, P.O. Box HH, Independence, MO 64055

Exercise 16
(worksheet _____)

Name: _____

WARNING SIGN MANAGEMENT

1. *Summary Title:* What is the warning sign you are learning to manage?

_____

2. *Past Experience of Ineffective Management:* Please describe a past experience with this warning sign during which you were sober and managed it ineffectively.

_____

_____

_____

_____

_____

3. *New Management Strategy:* If you had to experience this same situation again, what would you do differently to manage the warning sign more effectively?

_____

_____

_____

_____

_____

4. What were the constructive thoughts that helped you manage this warning sign effectively?

_____

_____

_____

_____

_____

5. What were the self-defeating thoughts that caused you to manage this warning sign ineffectively?

_____

_____

_____

_____

_____

6. What did you feel when you imagined yourself managing the warning sign effectively?

_____

_____

_____

_____

_____

7. What did you feel when you managed this warning sign ineffectively?

_____

_____

_____

_____

_____

8. What were the constructive behaviors that helped you to manage this warning sign effectively?

_____

_____

_____

_____

_____

_____

9. What were the self-defeating behaviors that caused you to manage this warning sign ineffectively?

_____

_____

_____

_____

_____

_____

10. *Action Plan:* Please describe an action plan that could be used to successfully manage this warning sign in the future. (Be sure to include strategies for constructive thinking, emotional management, behavior change, and situational management.)

_____

_____

_____

_____

_____

_____

_____

11. *Skills Needed:* What skills will you need to develop to be able to implement the action you described above?

_____

_____

_____

_____

_____

_____

_____

_____

_____

_____

_____

_____

The Staying Sober Workbook by Terence T. Gorski
Available from: Independence Press, P.O. Box HH, Independence, MO 64055

Name: _____

WARNING SIGN MANAGEMENT

1. *Summary Title:* What is the warning sign you are learning to manage?

_____

2. *Past Experience of Ineffective Management:* Please describe a past experience with this warning sign during which you were sober and managed it ineffectively.

_____

_____

_____

_____

_____

3. *New Management Strategy:* If you had to experience this same situation again, what would you do differently to manage the warning sign more effectively?

_____

_____

_____

_____

_____

4. What were the constructive thoughts that helped you manage this warning sign effectively?

_____

_____

_____

_____

5. What were the self-defeating thoughts that caused you to manage this warning sign ineffectively?

_____

_____

_____

_____

6. What did you feel when you imagined yourself managing the warning sign effectively?

_____

_____

_____

_____

7. What did you feel when you managed this warning sign ineffectively?

_____

_____

_____

_____

8. What were the constructive behaviors that helped you to manage this warning sign effectively?

_____

_____

_____

_____

_____

_____

9. What were the self-defeating behaviors that caused you to manage this warning sign ineffectively?

_____

_____

_____

_____

_____

_____

10. **Action Plan:** Please describe an action plan that could be used to successfully manage this warning sign in the future. (Be sure to include strategies for constructive thinking, emotional management, behavior change, and situational management.)

_____

_____

_____

_____

_____

_____

11. **Skills Needed:** What skills will you need to develop to be able to implement the action you described above?

_____

_____

_____

_____

_____

_____

_____

_____

_____

_____

_____

_____

The Staying Sober Workbook by Terence T. Gorski
Available from: Independence Press, P.O. Box HH, Independence, MO 64055

Name: _____

WARNING SIGN MANAGEMENT

1. *Summary Title:* What is the warning sign you are learning to manage?

   _____

2. *Past Experience of Ineffective Management:* Please describe a past experience with this warning sign during which you were sober and managed it ineffectively.

   _____

   _____

   _____

   _____

   _____

3. *New Management Strategy:* If you had to experience this same situation again, what would you do differently to manage the warning sign more effectively?

   _____

   _____

   _____

   _____

   _____

4. What were the constructive thoughts that helped you manage this warning sign effectively?

   _____

   _____

   _____

   _____

   _____

5. What were the self-defeating thoughts that caused you to manage this warning sign ineffectively?

   _____

   _____

   _____

   _____

   _____

6. What did you feel when you imagined yourself managing the warning sign effectively?

   _____

   _____

   _____

   _____

   _____

7. What did you feel when you managed this warning sign ineffectively?

   _____

   _____

   _____

   _____

   _____

8. What were the constructive behaviors that helped you to manage this warning sign effectively?

_____

_____

_____

_____

_____

9. What were the self-defeating behaviors that caused you to manage this warning sign ineffectively?

_____

_____

_____

_____

_____

10. **Action Plan:** Please describe an action plan that could be used to successfully manage this warning sign in the future. (Be sure to include strategies for constructive thinking, emotional management, behavior change, and situational management.)

_____

_____

_____

_____

_____

_____

_____

11. **Skills Needed:** What skills will you need to develop to be able to implement the action you described above?

_____

_____

_____

_____

_____

_____

_____

_____

_____

_____

_____

_____

The Staying Sober Workbook by Terence T. Gorski
Available from: Independence Press, P.O. Box HH, Independence, MO 64055

Name: _____

WARNING SIGN MANAGEMENT

1. **Summary Title:** What is the warning sign you are learning to manage?

   _____

2. **Past Experience of Ineffective Management:** Please describe a past experience with this warning sign during which you were sober and managed it ineffectively.

   _____
   _____
   _____
   _____
   _____

3. **New Management Strategy:** If you had to experience this same situation again, what would you do differently to manage the warning sign more effectively?

   _____
   _____
   _____
   _____
   _____

4. What were the constructive thoughts that helped you manage this warning sign effectively?

   _____
   _____
   _____
   _____

5. What were the self-defeating thoughts that caused you to manage this warning sign ineffectively?

   _____
   _____
   _____
   _____

6. What did you feel when you imagined yourself managing the warning sign effectively?

   _____
   _____
   _____
   _____

7. What did you feel when you managed this warning sign ineffectively?

   _____
   _____
   _____
   _____

8. What were the constructive behaviors that helped you to manage this warning sign effectively?

_____

_____

_____

_____

_____

_____

9. What were the self-defeating behaviors that caused you to manage this warning sign ineffectively?

_____

_____

_____

_____

_____

_____

10. **Action Plan:** Please describe an action plan that could be used to successfully manage this warning sign in the future. (Be sure to include strategies for constructive thinking, emotional management, behavior change, and situational management.)

_____

_____

_____

_____

_____

_____

11. **Skills Needed:** What skills will you need to develop to be able to implement the action you described above?

_____

_____

_____

_____

_____

_____

_____

_____

_____

_____

_____

The Staying Sober Workbook by Terence T. Gorski
Available from: Independence Press, P.O. Box HH, Independence, MO 64055

Exercise 16
(worksheet _____)

WARNING SIGN MANAGEMENT

1. *Summary Title:* What is the warning sign you are learning to manage?

   _____

2. *Past Experience of Ineffective Management:* Please describe a past experience with this warning sign during which you were sober and managed it ineffectively.

   _____

   _____

   _____

   _____

   _____

3. *New Management Strategy:* If you had to experience this same situation again, what would you do differently to manage the warning sign more effectively?

   _____

   _____

   _____

   _____

   _____

4. What were the constructive thoughts that helped you manage this warning sign effectively?

   _____

   _____

   _____

   _____

   _____

5. What were the self-defeating thoughts that caused you to manage this warning sign ineffectively?

   _____

   _____

   _____

   _____

   _____

6. What did you feel when you imagined yourself managing the warning sign effectively?

   _____

   _____

   _____

   _____

   _____

7. What did you feel when you managed this warning sign ineffectively?

   _____

   _____

   _____

   _____

   _____

8. What were the constructive behaviors that helped you to manage this warning sign effectively?

9. What were the self-defeating behaviors that caused you to manage this warning sign ineffectively?

10. *Action Plan:* Please describe an action plan that could be used to successfully manage this warning sign in the future. (Be sure to include strategies for constructive thinking, emotional management, behavior change, and situational management.)

11. *Skills Needed:* What skills will you need to develop to be able to implement the action you described above?

The Staying Sober Workbook by Terence T. Gorski
Available from: Independence Press, P.O. Box HH, Independence, MO 64055

Name: _____

WARNING SIGN MANAGEMENT

1. *Summary Title:* What is the warning sign you are learning to manage?

   _____

2. *Past Experience of Ineffective Management:* Please describe a past experience with this warning sign during which you were sober and managed it ineffectively.

   _____

   _____

   _____

   _____

3. *New Management Strategy:* If you had to experience this same situation again, what would you do differently to manage the warning sign more effectively?

   _____

   _____

   _____

   _____

   _____

4. What were the constructive thoughts that helped you manage this warning sign effectively?

   _____

   _____

   _____

   _____

5. What were the self-defeating thoughts that caused you to manage this warning sign ineffectively?

   _____

   _____

   _____

   _____

6. What did you feel when you imagined yourself managing the warning sign effectively?

   _____

   _____

   _____

   _____

   _____

7. What did you feel when you managed this warning sign ineffectively?

   _____

   _____

   _____

   _____

   _____

8. What were the constructive behaviors that helped you to manage this warning sign effectively?

_____

_____

_____

_____

_____

_____

9. What were the self-defeating behaviors that caused you to manage this warning sign ineffectively?

_____

_____

_____

_____

_____

_____

10. *Action Plan:* Please describe an action plan that could be used to successfully manage this warning sign in the future. (Be sure to include strategies for constructive thinking, emotional management, behavior change, and situational management.)

_____

_____

_____

_____

_____

_____

11. *Skills Needed:* What skills will you need to develop to be able to implement the action you described above?

_____

_____

_____

_____

_____

_____

_____

_____

_____

_____

_____

_____

The Staying Sober Workbook by Terence T. Gorski
Available from: Independence Press, P.O. Box HH, Independence, MO 64055

Name: _____

WARNING SIGN MANAGEMENT

1. **Summary Title:** What is the warning sign you are learning to manage?

   _____

2. **Past Experience of Ineffective Management:** Please describe a past experience with this warning sign during which you were sober and managed it ineffectively.

   _____

   _____

   _____

   _____

   _____

3. **New Management Strategy:** If you had to experience this same situation again, what would you do differently to manage the warning sign more effectively?

   _____

   _____

   _____

   _____

   _____

4. What were the constructive thoughts that helped you manage this warning sign effectively?

   _____

   _____

   _____

   _____

5. What were the self-defeating thoughts that caused you to manage this warning sign ineffectively?

   _____

   _____

   _____

   _____

6. What did you feel when you imagined yourself managing the warning sign effectively?

   _____

   _____

   _____

   _____

   _____

7. What did you feel when you managed this warning sign ineffectively?

   _____

   _____

   _____

   _____

   _____

8. What were the constructive behaviors that helped you to manage this warning sign effectively?

_____

_____

_____

_____

_____

_____

9. What were the self-defeating behaviors that caused you to manage this warning sign ineffectively?

_____

_____

_____

_____

_____

_____

10. **Action Plan:** Please describe an action plan that could be used to successfully manage this warning sign in the future. (Be sure to include strategies for constructive thinking, emotional management, behavior change, and situational management.)

_____

_____

_____

_____

_____

_____

_____

11. **Skills Needed:** What skills will you need to develop to be able to implement the action you described above?

_____

_____

_____

_____

_____

_____

_____

_____

_____

_____

_____

_____

_____

The Staying Sober Workbook by Terence T. Gorski
Available from: Independence Press, P.O. Box HH, Independence, MO 64055

WARNING SIGN MANAGEMENT

1. *Summary Title:* What is the warning sign you are learning to manage?

   _____

2. *Past Experience of Ineffective Management:* Please describe a past experience with this warning sign during which you were sober and managed it ineffectively.

   _____

   _____

   _____

   _____

   _____

3. *New Management Strategy:* If you had to experience this same situation again, what would you do differently to manage the warning sign more effectively?

   _____

   _____

   _____

   _____

   _____

   _____

4. What were the constructive thoughts that helped you manage this warning sign effectively?

   _____

   _____

   _____

   _____

   _____

5. What were the self-defeating thoughts that caused you to manage this warning sign ineffectively?

   _____

   _____

   _____

   _____

   _____

6. What did you feel when you imagined yourself managing the warning sign effectively?

   _____

   _____

   _____

   _____

   _____

7. What did you feel when you managed this warning sign ineffectively?

   _____

   _____

   _____

   _____

   _____

8. What were the constructive behaviors that helped you to manage this warning sign effectively?

_____

_____

_____

_____

_____

9. What were the self-defeating behaviors that caused you to manage this warning sign ineffectively?

_____

_____

_____

_____

_____

10. *Action Plan:* Please describe an action plan that could be used to successfully manage this warning sign in the future. (Be sure to include strategies for constructive thinking, emotional management, behavior change, and situational management.)

_____

_____

_____

_____

_____

_____

11. *Skills Needed:* What skills will you need to develop to be able to implement the action you described above?

_____

_____

_____

_____

_____

_____

_____

_____

_____

_____

_____

_____

_____

The Staying Sober Workbook by Terence T. Gorski
Available from: Independence Press, P.O. Box HH, Independence, MO 64055

Exercise 16
(worksheet _____)

WARNING SIGN MANAGEMENT

1. **Summary Title:** What is the warning sign you are learning to manage?

   _____

2. **Past Experience of Ineffective Management:** Please describe a past experience with this warning sign during which you were sober and managed it ineffectively.

   _____

   _____

   _____

   _____

   _____

3. **New Management Strategy:** If you had to experience this same situation again, what would you do differently to manage the warning sign more effectively?

   _____

   _____

   _____

   _____

   _____

4. What were the constructive thoughts that helped you manage this warning sign effectively?

   _____

   _____

   _____

   _____

5. What were the self-defeating thoughts that caused you to manage this warning sign ineffectively?

   _____

   _____

   _____

   _____

6. What did you feel when you imagined yourself managing the warning sign effectively?

   _____

   _____

   _____

   _____

   _____

7. What did you feel when you managed this warning sign ineffectively?

   _____

   _____

   _____

   _____

   _____

8. What were the constructive behaviors that helped you to manage this warning sign effectively?

_____

_____

_____

_____

_____

9. What were the self-defeating behaviors that caused you to manage this warning sign ineffectively?

_____

_____

_____

_____

_____

10. *Action Plan:* Please describe an action plan that could be used to successfully manage this warning sign in the future. (Be sure to include strategies for constructive thinking, emotional management, behavior change, and situational management.)

_____

_____

_____

_____

_____

_____

_____

11. *Skills Needed:* What skills will you need to develop to be able to implement the action you described above?

_____

_____

_____

_____

_____

_____

_____

_____

_____

_____

_____

_____

The Staying Sober Workbook by Terence T. Gorski
Available from: Independence Press, P.O. Box HH, Independence, MO 64055

Name: _____

WARNING SIGN MANAGEMENT

1. *Summary Title:* What is the warning sign you are learning to manage?

   _____

2. *Past Experience of Ineffective Management:* Please describe a past experience with this warning sign during which you were sober and managed it ineffectively.

   _____

   _____

   _____

   _____

   _____

3. *New Management Strategy:* If you had to experience this same situation again, what would you do differently to manage the warning sign more effectively?

   _____

   _____

   _____

   _____

   _____

4. What were the constructive thoughts that helped you manage this warning sign effectively?

   _____

   _____

   _____

   _____

5. What were the self-defeating thoughts that caused you to manage this warning sign ineffectively?

   _____

   _____

   _____

   _____

6. What did you feel when you imagined yourself managing the warning sign effectively?

   _____

   _____

   _____

   _____

   _____

7. What did you feel when you managed this warning sign ineffectively?

   _____

   _____

   _____

   _____

   _____

8. What were the constructive behaviors that helped you to manage this warning sign effectively?

_____

_____

_____

_____

_____

9. What were the self-defeating behaviors that caused you to manage this warning sign ineffectively?

_____

_____

_____

_____

_____

10. **Action Plan:** Please describe an action plan that could be used to successfully manage this warning sign in the future. (Be sure to include strategies for constructive thinking, emotional management, behavior change, and situational management.)

_____

_____

_____

_____

_____

_____

_____

11. **Skills Needed:** What skills will you need to develop to be able to implement the action you described above?

_____

_____

_____

_____

_____

_____

_____

_____

_____

_____

_____

The Staying Sober Workbook by Terence T. Gorski
Available from: Independence Press, P.O. Box HH, Independence, MO 64055

Exercise 16
(worksheet _____)

Name: _____

WARNING SIGN MANAGEMENT

1. *Summary Title:* What is the warning sign you are learning to manage?

   _____

2. *Past Experience of Ineffective Management:* Please describe a past experience with this warning sign during which you were sober and managed it ineffectively.

   _____

   _____

   _____

   _____

   _____

3. *New Management Strategy:* If you had to experience this same situation again, what would you do differently to manage the warning sign more effectively?

   _____

   _____

   _____

   _____

   _____

4. What were the constructive thoughts that helped you manage this warning sign effectively?

   _____

   _____

   _____

   _____

   _____

5. What were the self-defeating thoughts that caused you to manage this warning sign ineffectively?

   _____

   _____

   _____

   _____

   _____

6. What did you feel when you imagined yourself managing the warning sign effectively?

   _____

   _____

   _____

   _____

   _____

7. What did you feel when you managed this warning sign ineffectively?

   _____

   _____

   _____

   _____

   _____

8. What were the constructive behaviors that helped you to manage this warning sign effectively?

_____

_____

_____

_____

_____

_____

9. What were the self-defeating behaviors that caused you to manage this warning sign ineffectively?

_____

_____

_____

_____

_____

_____

10. *Action Plan:* Please describe an action plan that could be used to successfully manage this warning sign in the future. (Be sure to include strategies for constructive thinking, emotional management, behavior change, and situational management.)

_____

_____

_____

_____

_____

_____

_____

11. *Skills Needed:* What skills will you need to develop to be able to implement the action you described above?

_____

_____

_____

_____

_____

_____

_____

_____

_____

_____

_____

_____

The Staying Sober Workbook by Terence T. Gorski
Available from: Independence Press, P.O. Box HH, Independence, MO 64055

Exercise 17

PATIENT NAME _____

THERAPIST _____

DATE _____

THE HIGH RISK SITUATION LIST

Copyright, T. Gorski, 1985

High Risk Situation 1: Title: _____

Description: I am most likely to experience relapse warning signs when:

_____

_____

_____

High Risk Situation 2: Title: _____

Description: I am most likely to experience relapse warning signs when:

_____

_____

_____

High Risk Situation 3: Title: _____

Description: I am most likely to experience relapse warning signs when:

_____

_____

_____

High Risk Situation 4: Title: _____

Description: I am most likely to experience relapse warning signs when:

_____

_____

_____

High Risk Situation 5: Title: _____

Description: I am most likely to experience relapse warning signs when:

_____

_____

_____

The Staying Sober Workbook by Terence T. Gorski
Available from: Independence Press, P.O. Box HH, Independence, MO 64055

**Exercise 18
(worksheet #1)**

PATIENT NAME _____

THERAPIST _____

DATE _____

THE HIGH RISK SITUATION WORKSHEET

Copyright, T. Gorski, 1985

INSTRUCTIONS: Select a high risk situation from the High Risk Situation List and answer the questions below.

1. The high risk situation I am going to work with:

   _____

2. The three major relapse warning signs from my Final Warning Sign List that could be activated by this high risk situation are:

A. _____

B. _____

C. _____

2. List three self-defeating ways that you have used in the past to cope with this high-risk situation.

A. _____

_____

B. _____

_____

C. _____

_____

3. List three methods of coping with the high risk situation that you believe could be effective in the future.

A. _____

_____

B. _____

_____

C. _____

_____

The Staying Sober Workbook **by Terence T. Gorski**
Available from: Independence Press, P.O. Box HH, Independence, MO 64055

**Exercise 18
(worksheet #2)**

PATIENT NAME _____

THERAPIST _____

DATE _____

THE HIGH RISK SITUATION WORKSHEET

Copyright, T. Gorski, 1985

INSTRUCTIONS: Select a high risk situation from the High Risk Situation List and answer the questions below.

1. The high risk situation I am going to work with:

   _____

2. The three major relapse warning signs from my Final Warning Sign List that could be activated by this high risk situation are:

A. _____

B. _____

C. _____

2. List three self-defeating ways that you have used in the past to cope with this high-risk situation.

A. _____

   _____

B. _____

   _____

C. _____

   _____

3. List three methods of coping with the high risk situation that you believe could be effective in the future.

A. _____

   _____

B. _____

   _____

C. _____

   _____

The Staying Sober Workbook by Terence T. Gorski
Available from: Independence Press, P.O. Box HH, Independence, MO 64055

**Exercise 18
(worksheet #3)**

PATIENT NAME _____

THERAPIST _____

DATE _____

THE HIGH RISK SITUATION WORKSHEET

Copyright, T. Gorski, 1985

INSTRUCTIONS: Select a high risk situation from the High Risk Situation List and answer the questions below.

1. The high risk situation I am going to work with:

   _____

2. The three major relapse warning signs from my Final Warning Sign List that could be activated by this high risk situation are:

A. _____

B. _____

C. _____

2. List three self-defeating ways that you have used in the past to cope with this high-risk situation.

A. _____

   _____

B. _____

   _____

C. _____

   _____

3. List three methods of coping with the high risk situation that you believe could be effective in the future.

A. _____

   _____

B. _____

   _____

C. _____

   _____

The Staying Sober Workbook by Terence T. Gorski
Available from: Independence Press, P.O. Box HH, Independence, MO 64055

Exercise 18
(worksheet #4)

PATIENT NAME _____

THERAPIST _____

DATE _____

THE HIGH RISK SITUATION WORKSHEET

Copyright, T. Gorski, 1985

INSTRUCTIONS: Select a high risk situation from the High Risk Situation List and answer the questions below.

1. The high risk situation I am going to work with:

_____

2. The three major relapse warning signs from my Final Warning Sign List that could be activated by this high risk situation are:

A. _____

B. _____

C. _____

2. List three self-defeating ways that you have used in the past to cope with this high-risk situation.

A. _____

_____

B. _____

_____

C. _____

_____

3. List three methods of coping with the high risk situation that you believe could be effective in the future.

A. _____

_____

B. _____

_____

C. _____

_____

The Staying Sober Workbook by Terence T. Gorski
Available from: Independence Press, P.O. Box HH, Independence, MO 64055

**Exercise 18
(worksheet #5)**

PATIENT NAME _____

THERAPIST _____

DATE _____

THE HIGH RISK SITUATION WORKSHEET

Copyright, T. Gorski, 1985

INSTRUCTIONS: Select a high risk situation from the High Risk Situation List and answer the questions below.

1. The high risk situation I am going to work with:

_____

2. The three major relapse warning signs from my Final Warning Sign List that could be activated by this high risk situation are:

A. _____

B. _____

C. _____

2. List three self-defeating ways that you have used in the past to cope with this high-risk situation.

A. _____

_____

B. _____

_____

C. _____

_____

3. List three methods of coping with the high risk situation that you believe could be effective in the future.

A. _____

_____

B. _____

_____

C. _____

_____

The Staying Sober Workbook by Terence T. Gorski
Available from: Independence Press, P.O. Box HH, Independence, MO 64055

Exercise 19

PATIENT NAME _____

THERAPIST _____

DATE _____

THE EARLY INTERVENTION WORKSHEET

Copyright, T. Gorski, 1985

1. Please describe what actions you will take if you return to addictive use and experience a moment of sanity where you have the power to make a choice.

_____

_____

_____

_____

_____

_____

_____

2. Please describe what you would expect others to do to help you if you returned to addictive use.

_____

_____

_____

_____

_____

_____

_____

_____

_____

_____

_____

_____

_____

_____

3. If you returned to addictive use and others attempted to get you into treatment and you refused, what do you believe would be the most effective strategies for forcing you into treatment even if you didn't want to go?

_____

_____

_____

_____

_____

_____

_____

_____

_____

_____

_____

_____

_____

_____

_____

_____

_____

_____

_____

_____

_____

_____

It is strongly recommended that you give a copy of this form to your counselor, family doctor, personal attorney, sponsor, family members, and other members of your relapse prevention network.

The Staying Sober Workbook by Terence T. Gorski
Available from: Independence Press, P.O. Box HH, Independence, MO 64055

Exercise 20   Name: _____

THE DAILY PLANNING GUIDE

Day _____ Date _____ Time _____

MAJOR GOALS FOR TODAY:

☐ 1. _____

☐ 2. _____

☐ 3. _____

☐ 4. _____

☐ 5. _____

RECOVERY TASKS

☐ 1. _____

☐ 2. _____

☐ 3. _____

☐ 4. _____

☐ 5. _____

DAILY TASKS

☐ 1. _____

☐ 2. _____

☐ 3. _____

☐ 4. _____

☐ 5. _____

☐ 6. _____

☐ 7. _____

☐ 8. _____

☐ 9. _____

☐ 10. _____

DAILY TIME PLAN

A M   6:00– 7:00 _____

      7:00– 8:00 _____

      8:00– 9:00 _____

      9:00–10:00 _____

      10:00–11:00 _____

      11:00–12:00 _____

P M   12:00– 1:00 _____

      1:00– 2:00 _____

      2:00– 3:00 _____

      3:00– 4:00 _____

      4:00– 5:00 _____

      5:00– 6:00 _____

E V E N I N G _____

_____

_____

_____

Notes: _____

_____

The Staying Sober Workbook by Terence T. Gorski
Available from: Independence Press, P.O. Box HH, Independence, MO 64055

Exercise 21   Name: _____

THE EVENING REVIEW INVENTORY

Day _____ Date _____ Time _____

1. *PERSONAL AND PROFESSIONAL PROGRESS:*
A. Did I make progress today toward the accomplishment of my personal and professional goals?
   ☐ Yes.   ☐ No.   ☐ Uncertain.

B. How do I feel about that progress?

   _____

   _____

2. *PERSONAL AND PROFESSIONAL SHORTCOMINGS:*
A. Did I encounter problems today in making progress toward my personal and professional goals?
   ☐ Yes.   ☐ No.   ☐ Uncertain.

B. How do I feel about those problems?

   _____

   _____

3. *ACTIVE WARNING SIGNS:*
A. Did I experience warning signs of excessive stress or relapse?
   ☐ Yes.   ☐ No.   ☐ Uncertain.

B. What have I done to manage those warning signs?

   _____

   _____

C. How do I feel about the presence of those warning signs?

   _____

   _____

4. *DECISION ABOUT THE NEED FOR OUTSIDE HELP:*
A. Do I need to talk with someone about the events of the day?
   ☐ Yes.   ☐ No.   ☐ Uncertain.

B. Do I need outside help to deal with the problems or warning signs that I experienced today?
   ☐ Yes.   ☐ No.   ☐ Uncertain.

C. What feelings am I experiencing as I think about my need for outside help?

   _____

   _____

The Staying Sober Workbook by Terence T. Gorski
Available from: Independence Press, P.O. Box HH, Independence, MO 64055

Exercise 22

Name: _____

Date: _____

THE RECOVERY QUESTIONNAIRE

INSTRUCTIONS: Please answer the following questions. Think carefully about what you did to manage your recovery during your last efforts to stay sober.

_____ 1. How often did you attend group or individual counseling sessions?

☐ Never (0)   ☐ Sometimes (1)   ☐ Often (2)   ☐ Very Often (3)

Please describe the type of counseling you participated in and your personal reaction to that counseling:

_____

_____

_____

_____

_____ 2. How often did you regularly attend AA or self-help group meetings?

☐ Never (0)   ☐ Sometimes (1)   ☐ Often (2)   ☐ Very Often (3)

A. How many meetings per week did you attend? _____

B. What type of meetings did you attend?

☐ Open   ☐ Closed   ☐ Speaker   ☐ Discussion

C. Did you have a home group?   ☐ Yes   ☐ No

D. Please describe your personal reaction to the meetings:

_____

_____

_____

_____

_____

_____

_____

_____

_____ 3. How often did you talk with your sponsor in your Twelve Step self-help group (AA, NA, etc.)? If you did not have a sponsor, check never.

☐ Never (0)　　☐ Sometimes (1)　　☐ Often (2)　　☐ Very Often (3)

If you had a sponsor, please describe your relationship with him or her and the good points and bad points of that relationship.

_____

_____

_____

_____

_____

_____ 4. The following is a list of the Twelve Steps of AA. Read each step and place a check in the answer that most clearly describes your past completion of that task. If you are not familiar with the Twelve Steps or would like more detailed guidelines about what is required to complete them, refer to Appendix B and complete the Questionnaire of Twelve Step Completion.

		Fully Completed	Partially Completed	Did Not Start
A.	Step 1	☐ (2)	☐ (1)	☐ (0)
B.	Step 2	☐ (2)	☐ (1)	☐ (0)
C.	Step 3	☐ (2)	☐ (1)	☐ (0)
D.	Step 4	☐ (2)	☐ (1)	☐ (0)
E.	Step 5	☐ (2)	☐ (1)	☐ (0)
F.	Step 6	☐ (2)	☐ (1)	☐ (0)
G.	Step 7	☐ (2)	☐ (1)	☐ (0)
H.	Step 8	☐ (2)	☐ (1)	☐ (0)
I.	Step 9	☐ (2)	☐ (1)	☐ (0)
J.	Step 10	☐ (2)	☐ (1)	☐ (0)
K.	Step 11	☐ (2)	☐ (1)	☐ (0)
L.	Step 12	☐ (2)	☐ (1)	☐ (0)

Please describe how you felt about working the steps—which steps you found helpful and those you found not to be helpful.

_____

_____

_____

_____

_____

_____

_____

_____

_____ 5. How frequently did you eat three well-balanced meals per day?

☐ Never (0)　　☐ Sometimes (1)　　☐ Often (2)　　☐ Very Often (3)

Please describe an average daily eating plan.

Breakfast: _____

Morning Snack: _____

Lunch: _____

Afternoon Snack: _____

Dinner: _____

Evening Snack: _____

Other: _____

_____ 6. How often did you avoid foods high in sugars (candy, chocolate, cakes, etc.)?

☐ Never (0)　　☐ Sometimes (1)　　☐ Often (2)　　☐ Very Often (3)

Please describe your favorite high-sugar or binge foods, and how you feel before, during, and after an episode of heavy eating.

_____

_____

_____

_____ 7. How often did you use beverages containing caffeine?

☐ Never (3)　　☐ Sometimes (2)　　☐ Often (1)　　☐ Very Often (0)

A. How much caffeine would you consume in a normal day?

☐ Cups of coffee　　　　　　　　　= _____.
☐ Cans of caffeinated beverages　= _____.
☐ Other: Specify:_____　= _____.

B. How often did you notice a change in mood (becoming more stimulated, energized, alert, or wired) as a result of your use of caffeine?

☐ Never (0)　　☐ Sometimes (1)　　☐ Often (2)　　☐ Very Often (3)

_____ 8. How often did you use nicotine (including cigarettes, cigars, and smokeless tobacco)?

☐ Never (3)　　☐ Sometimes (2)　　☐ Often (1)　　☐ Very Often (0)

_____ 9. How often did you exercise at least 3 times per week for a minimum period of 20 to 30 minutes in a manner that was strenuous enough to make you breathe hard and begin to sweat?

☐ Never (0)　　☐ Sometimes (1)　　☐ Often (2)　　☐ Very Often (3)

Please describe your regular exercise habits:

_____

_____

_____ 10. How often have you used relaxation techniques?

☐ Never (0)　　　☐ Sometimes (1)　　　☐ Often (2)　　　☐ Very Often (3)

Please check the type and frequency of relaxation exercises that you used.

Type of Relaxation Exercise Used:	Never	Sometimes	Often	Very Often
1. Breathing exercises.	☐	☐	☐	☐
2. Muscle relaxation.	☐	☐	☐	☐
3. Guided imagery.	☐	☐	☐	☐
4. Conscious relaxation of various parts of your body.	☐	☐	☐	☐
5. Biofeedback.	☐	☐	☐	☐

Frequency Used:

_____ 11. How often did you use prayer and/or meditation on a regular basis to help you recover?

☐ Never (0)　　　☐ Sometimes (1)　　　☐ Often (2)　　　☐ Very Often (3)

Please describe the types of prayer and/or meditation you found most helpful and least helpful:

_____

_____

_____

_____ 12. How frequently did you talk with people about your life and ask for feedback on a regular basis?

☐ Never (0)　　　☐ Sometimes (1)　　　☐ Often (2)　　　☐ Very Often (3)

Please describe the primary people that you talked to and what you talked to them about:

_____

_____

_____

_____

_____ 13. How often did you attempt to solve problems promptly as they came up?

☐ Never (0)　　　☐ Sometimes (1)　　　☐ Often (2)　　　☐ Very Often (3)

A. Please describe the type of problems you attempted to solve promptly as they came up:

_____

_____

_____
_____
_____

B. Please describe the types of problems you tended to put off solving.

_____
_____
_____
_____

_____ 14. How often did you schedule time for recreational activities (recreational activities are activities that you consider to be fun)?

☐ Never (0) ☐ Sometimes (1) ☐ Often (2) ☐ Very Often (3)

A. Please describe the recreational activities that you most enjoyed:

_____
_____
_____
_____
_____

B. Please describe the recreational activities that you least enjoyed and why you didn't enjoy them:

_____
_____
_____
_____
_____

_____ 15. How often did you schedule time for activities with your family?

☐ Never (0) ☐ Sometimes (1) ☐ Often (2) ☐ Very Often (3)

Please describe your current relationship with the members of your family. Describe how your addiction and tendency to relapse has affected your relationship with your family.

_____
_____
_____
_____

_____ 16. How often did you schedule time to spend with friends?

☐ Never (0)   ☐ Sometimes (1)   ☐ Often (2)   ☐ Very Often (3)

Please list the current friends you have and how close you feel to them:

_____

_____

_____

_____

_____ 17. How often did you work on a regular schedule that didn't interfere with recreational or treatment activities?

☐ Never (0)   ☐ Sometimes (1)   ☐ Often (2)   ☐ Very Often (3)

Please describe your typical work week. If you tend to overwork (work more than 8 hours per day or 40 hours per week, please describe how many hours and why you work that hard).

_____

_____

_____

_____

_____

_____ 18. How often did you schedule some quiet time to think and plan your recovery program on a regular basis?

☐ Never (0)   ☐ Sometimes (1)   ☐ Often (2)   ☐ Very Often (3)

Please describe your feelings and reactions to planning periods of quiet time for yourself and your recovery:

_____

_____

_____

_____

_____

The degree to which the lack of recovery-support activities contributed to your relapse can be roughly evaluated by counting the number of points scored in answering the above questions. Next to each multiple choice answer is a numeric score. Add all of those scores together and place your total score below.

TOTAL SCORE = _____ out of 78.

The scoring and interpretation key can be found in Appendix A, page 159 of this exercise manual.

The Staying Sober Workbook by Terence T. Gorski
Available from: Independence Press, P.O. Box HH, Independence, MO 64055

Name: _____

EVALUATION OF STRENGTHS AND WEAKNESSES

Strengths in Past Recovery Programs: What things did you do in your past recovery programs that were helpful and can act as a foundation as you plan a new and more effective program?

_____

_____

_____

_____

_____

_____

_____

_____

_____

_____

Weaknesses in Past Recovery Programs: What things did you do or fail to do in your recovery program that weakened you or set you up to relapse?

_____

_____

_____

_____

_____

_____

_____

_____

_____

_____

_____

_____

The Staying Sober Workbook by Terence T. Gorski
Available from: Independence Press, P.O. Box HH, Independence, MO 64055

Name: _____

EVALUATION OF LEVELS OF EXPECTANCY

1. Did you expect too much of yourself and attempt to do too much too fast in your previous recovery efforts?

   ☐ Yes   ☐ No

   Please explain why you answered the question as you did:

   _____

   _____

   _____

2. Did you expect too little of yourself and fail to put into practice the basics of recovery?

   ☐ Yes   ☐ No

   Please explain why you answered the question as you did:

   _____

   _____

   _____

3. Did you attempt to do the wrong kinds of things in your previous recovery efforts? In other words did you focus on the easy aspects of recovery by doing things that made you look good while avoiding or denying the more difficult aspects of recovery which would address your major problems?

   ☐ Yes   ☐ No

   Please explain why you answered the question as you did:

   _____

   _____

   _____

4. Please list the things you will need to do differently in your recovery if you are to avoid relapse in the future.

   _____

   _____

   _____

   _____

   _____

   _____

   _____

   _____

The Staying Sober Workbook by Terence T. Gorski
Available from: Independence Press, P.O. Box HH, Independence, MO 64055

RECOVERY PROGRAM
STANDARD RECOMMENDATIONS

Instructions: The following questions are designed to help you plan your ongoing recovery. Nineteen key recovery recommendations are reviewed. Each standard recommendation is followed by three questions. Answer each question as honestly as you can.

1. **Professional Counseling:**

   A. **Belief in need.** How strongly do you believe that you need to attend regular group and individual sessions in order to avoid relapse in the future?

   ☐ 1. Very strongly   ☐ 3. Not very strongly

   ☐ 2. Strongly   ☐ 4. Not at all strongly

   B. **Obstacles.** What obstacles are likely to prevent you from attending regular group and individual counseling sessions?

   _____

   _____

   C. **Likelihood.** How likely are you to attend regular group or individual counseling sessions in the future?

   ☐ 1. Very likely   ☐ 3. Not very likely

   ☐ 2. Somewhat likely   ☐ 4. Not at all likely

2. **Self-Help Groups:**

   A. **Belief in need.** How strongly do you believe that you need to attend self-help groups in order to avoid relapse in the future?

   ☐ 1. Very strongly   ☐ 3. Not very strongly

   ☐ 2. Strongly   ☐ 4. Not at all strongly

   B. **Obstacles.** What obstacles are likely to prevent you from attending self-help groups?

   _____

   _____

   C. **Likelihood.** How likely are you to regularly attend self-help groups in the future?

   ☐ 1. Very likely   ☐ 3. Not very likely

   ☐ 2. Somewhat likely   ☐ 4. Not at all likely

3. **Sponsorship:**

   A. **Belief in need.** How strongly do you believe that you need sponsorship in order to avoid relapse in the future?

   ☐ 1. Very strongly　　　　　　　☐ 3. Not very strongly

   ☐ 2. Strongly　　　　　　　　　☐ 4. Not at all strongly

   B. **Obstacles.** What obstacles are likely to prevent you from sponsorship?

   _____

   _____

   C. **Likelihood.** How likely are you to have a sponsor with whom you talk on a regular basis in the future?

   ☐ 1. Very likely　　　　　　　　☐ 3. Not very likely

   ☐ 2. Somewhat likely　　　　　　☐ 4. Not at all likely

4. **Step Work:**

   A. **Belief in need.** How strongly do you believe that you need step work in order to avoid relapse in the future?

   ☐ 1. Very strongly　　　　　　　☐ 3. Not very strongly

   ☐ 2. Strongly　　　　　　　　　☐ 4. Not at all strongly

   B. **Obstacles.** What obstacles are likely to prevent you from step work?

   _____

   _____

   C. **Likelihood.** How likely are you to use step work in the future?

   ☐ 1. Very likely　　　　　　　　☐ 3. Not very likely

   ☐ 2. Somewhat likely　　　　　　☐ 4. Not at all likely

5. **Meal Plan:**

   A. **Belief in need.** How strongly do you believe that you need a meal plan in order to avoid relapse in the future?

   ☐ 1. Very strongly　　　　　　　☐ 3. Not very strongly

   ☐ 2. Strongly　　　　　　　　　☐ 4. Not at all strongly

   B. **Obstacles.** What obstacles are likely to prevent you from a meal plan?

   _____

   _____

   C. **Likelihood.** How likely are you to eat three well-balanced meals per day in the future?

   ☐ 1. Very likely　　　　　　　　☐ 3. Not very likely

   ☐ 2. Somewhat likely　　　　　　☐ 4. Not at all likely

6. **Avoiding Sugars:**

A. **Belief in need.** How strongly do you believe that you need to avoid sugars in order to avoid relapse in the future?

☐ 1. Very strongly

☐ 3. Not very strongly

☐ 2. Strongly

☐ 4. Not at all strongly

B. **Obstacles.** What obstacles are likely to prevent you from avoiding sugars?

_____

_____

C. **Likelihood.** How likely are you to avoid foods high in sugars in the future?

☐ 1. Very likely

☐ 3. Not very likely

☐ 2. Somewhat likely

☐ 4. Not at all likely

7. **Avoiding Caffeine:**

A. **Belief in need.** How strongly do you believe that you need to avoid caffeine in order to avoid relapse in the future?

☐ 1. Very strongly

☐ 3. Not very strongly

☐ 2. Strongly

☐ 4. Not at all strongly

B. **Obstacles.** What obstacles are likely to prevent you from avoiding beverages containing caffeine?

_____

_____

C. **Likelihood.** How likely are you to avoid beverages containing caffeine in the future?

☐ 1. Very likely

☐ 3. Not very likely

☐ 2. Somewhat likely

☐ 4. Not at all likely

8. **Avoiding Nicotine:**

A. **Belief in need.** How strongly do you believe that you need to avoid nicotine in order to avoid relapse in the future?

☐ 1. Very strongly

☐ 3. Not very strongly

☐ 2. Strongly

☐ 4. Not at all strongly

B. **Obstacles.** What obstacles are likely to prevent you from avoiding nicotine?

_____

_____

C. **Likelihood.** How likely are you to avoid the use of nicotine (including cigarettes, cigars, and smokeless tobacco in the future?

☐ 1. Very likely

☐ 3. Not very likely

☐ 2. Somewhat likely

☐ 4. Not at all likely

9. **Regular Exercise:**
   A. **Belief in need.** How strongly do you believe that you need regular exercise in order to avoid relapse in the future?

   ☐ 1. Very strongly   ☐ 3. Not very strongly

   ☐ 2. Strongly   ☐ 4. Not at all strongly

   B. **Obstacles.** What obstacles are likely to prevent you from regular exercise?

   _____

   _____

   C. **Likelihood.** In the future how likely are you to exercise at least three times per week for a minimum period of 20 to 30 minutes in a manner that is strenuous enough to make you breathe hard and begin to sweat?

   ☐ 1. Very likely   ☐ 3. Not very likely

   ☐ 2. Somewhat likely   ☐ 4. Not at all likely

10. **Relaxation Exercises:**
    A. **Belief in need.** How strongly do you believe that you need relaxation exercises in order to avoid relapse in the future?

    ☐ 1. Very strongly   ☐ 3. Not very strongly

    ☐ 2. Strongly   ☐ 4. Not at all strongly

    B. **Obstacles.** What obstacles are likely to prevent you from relaxation exercises?

    _____

    _____

    C. **Likelihood.** How likely are you to use relaxation techniques to relax in the future?

    ☐ 1. Very likely   ☐ 3. Not very likely

    ☐ 2. Somewhat likely   ☐ 4. Not at all likely

11. **Prayer and Meditation:**
    A. **Belief in need.** How strongly do you believe that you need prayer and meditation in order to avoid relapse in the future?

    ☐ 1. Very strongly   ☐ 3. Not very strongly

    ☐ 2. Strongly   ☐ 4. Not at all strongly

    B. **Obstacles.** What obstacles are likely to prevent you from prayer and meditation?

    _____

    _____

    C. **Likelihood.** How likely are you to use prayer and meditation to help you recover in the future?

    ☐ 1. Very likely   ☐ 3. Not very likely

    ☐ 2. Somewhat likely   ☐ 4. Not at all likely

12. **Talking with Others:**

    A. **Belief in need.** How strongly do you believe that you need to talk with others in order to avoid relapse in the future?

        ☐ 1. Very strongly   ☐ 3. Not very strongly

        ☐ 2. Strongly   ☐ 4. Not at all strongly

    B. **Obstacles.** What obstacles are likely to prevent you from talking with others?

    _____

    _____

    C. **Likelihood.** How likely are you to talk to people about your life and ask for feedback in the future?

        ☐ 1. Very likely   ☐ 3. Not very likely

        ☐ 2. Somewhat likely   ☐ 4. Not at all likely

13. **Prompt Problem Solving:**

    A. **Belief in need.** How strongly do you believe that you need prompt problem solving in order to avoid relapse in the future?

        ☐ 1. Very strongly   ☐ 3. Not very strongly

        ☐ 2. Strongly   ☐ 4. Not at all strongly

    B. **Obstacles.** What obstacles are likely to prevent you from prompt problem solving?

    _____

    _____

    C. **Likelihood.** How likely are you to attempt to solve problems promptly as they come up in the future?

        ☐ 1. Very likely   ☐ 3. Not very likely

        ☐ 2. Somewhat likely   ☐ 4. Not at all likely

14. **Recreational Activities:**

    A. **Belief in need.** How strongly do you believe that you need recreational activities in order to avoid relapse in the future?

        ☐ 1. Very strongly   ☐ 3. Not very strongly

        ☐ 2. Strongly   ☐ 4. Not at all strongly

    B. **Obstacles.** What obstacles are likely to prevent you from recreational activities?

    _____

    _____

    C. **Likelihood.** How likely are you to schedule time for recreational activities in the future?

        ☐ 1. Very likely   ☐ 3. Not very likely

        ☐ 2. Somewhat likely   ☐ 4. Not at all likely

15. **Family Activities:**

   A. **Belief in need.** How strongly do you believe that you need family activities in order to avoid relapse in the future?

   ☐ 1. Very strongly   ☐ 3. Not very strongly

   ☐ 2. Strongly   ☐ 4. Not at all strongly

   B. **Obstacles.** What obstacles are likely to prevent you from family activities?

   _____

   _____

   C. **Likelihood.** How likely are you to schedule time for activities with your family in the future?

   ☐ 1. Very likely   ☐ 3. Not very likely

   ☐ 2. Somewhat likely   ☐ 4. Not at all likely

16. **Time with Friends:**

   A. **Belief in need.** How strongly do you believe that you need time with friends in order to avoid relapse in the future?

   ☐ 1. Very strongly   ☐ 3. Not very strongly

   ☐ 2. Strongly   ☐ 4. Not at all strongly

   B. **Obstacles.** What obstacles are likely to prevent you from time with friends?

   _____

   _____

   C. **Likelihood.** How likely are you to schedule time to spend with friends in the future?

   ☐ 1. Very likely   ☐ 3. Not very likely

   ☐ 2. Somewhat likely   ☐ 4. Not at all likely

17. **Reasonable Work Schedule:**

   A. **Belief in need.** How strongly do you believe that you need a reasonable work schedule in order to avoid relapse in the future?

   ☐ 1. Very strongly   ☐ 3. Not very strongly

   ☐ 2. Strongly   ☐ 4. Not at all strongly

   B. **Obstacles.** What obstacles are likely to prevent you from a reasonable work schedule?

   _____

   _____

   C. **Likelihood.** How likely are you to work on a regular schedule that doesn't interfere with recreational or recovery activities in the future?

   ☐ 1. Very likely   ☐ 3. Not very likely

   ☐ 2. Somewhat likely   ☐ 4. Not at all likely

18. **Quiet Time:**

    A. **Belief in need.** How strongly do you believe that you need quiet time in order to avoid relapse in the future?

        ☐ 1. Very strongly   ☐ 3. Not very strongly

        ☐ 2. Strongly   ☐ 4. Not at all strongly

    B. **Obstacles.** What obstacles are likely to prevent you from quiet time?

    _____

    _____

    C. **Likelihood.** How likely are you to schedule some quiet time to think and plan your recovery program in the future?

        ☐ 1. Very likely   ☐ 3. Not very likely

        ☐ 2. Somewhat likely   ☐ 4. Not at all likely

19. What are the recommendations that you are committing yourself to follow during this effort at recovery?

    I am making a commitment to myself to:

_____

_____

_____

_____

_____

_____

_____

_____

_____

_____

_____

_____

_____

_____

_____

The Staying Sober Workbook by Terence T. Gorski
Available from: Independence Press, P.O. Box HH, Independence, MO 64055

Exercise 26   **Name:** _____

RECOVERY GOALS

1. **Personal Goals.** Please identify three personal characteristics that need to be changed if you are to avoid relapse:

A. _____

_____

B. _____

_____

C. _____

_____

2. **Occupational Goals.** Please identify the three major professional problems that need to be resolved if you are to avoid relapse:

A. _____

_____

B. _____

_____

C. _____

_____

3. **Family Goals.** Please identify the three major family problems that need to be resolved if you are to avoid relapse:

A. _____

_____

B. _____

_____

C. _____

_____

4. **Social Goals.** Please identify the three major social problems that need to be resolved if you are to avoid relapse:

A. _____

_____

B. _____

_____

C. _____

_____
_____

5. **Twelve Step Goals.** Please identify the three major problems you have had in working your Twelve Step Program that will need to be resolved if you are to avoid relapse:

A. _____

_____

B. _____

_____

C. _____

_____
_____

The Staying Sober Workbook by Terence T. Gorski
Available from: Independence Press, P.O. Box HH, Independence, MO 64055

Exercise 27

PATIENT NAME _____

THERAPIST_____

DATE_____

RECOVERY ACTIVITIES PLANNING

SCHEDULE OF RECOVERY ACTIVITIES: Please list the days, times, and description of the recovery activities you plan to use to avoid future relapse.

1. PROFESSIONAL TREATMENT ACTIVITIES: Please describe the recovery activities you are going to complete under the supervision of a physician, therapist, or counselor such as medical checkups, group therapy, individual therapy, antabuse, family counseling, career counseling, etc.

DAY:	TIME:	ACTIVITY AND DESCRIPTION:

2. SELF-HELP GROUP INVOLVEMENT: Please describe the recovery activities that you plan to do with other people such as attending AA, NA, Al-Anon meetings, meetings with sponsor, phone calls, etc.

DAY:	TIME:	ACTIVITY AND DESCRIPTION:

3. SELF-CARE PROGRAM: Please describe the activities that you are going to complete by yourself in order to help your recovery. Include such things as recovery-oriented reading, working the steps, daily inventories, prayer, meditation, etc.

DAY:	TIME:	ACTIVITY AND DESCRIPTION:

4. PERSONAL FEELINGS AND REACTIONS: Please briefly describe your personal feelings and reactions to needing to implement the recovery program you outlined above. Remember that most recovering persons have mixed feelings about needing a recovery program. The inability to identify both positive and negative reactions to recovery planning may be a sign of denial.

_____

_____

_____

_____

_____

_____

_____

_____

_____

_____

_____

_____

_____

The Staying Sober Workbook by Terence T. Gorski
Available from: Independence Press, P.O. Box HH, Independence, MO 64055

PATIENT NAME _____

DATE _____

TESTING THE RECOVERY PROGRAM

Copyright, CENAPS Corporation, 1985

INSTRUCTIONS: Please list each of your relapse warning signs by number and summary title. Next to each describe the recovery-program activities listed on Exercise 15: The Final Warning Sign List that will help you prevent the warning sign from occurring or manage it if it does occur.

#	WARNING SIGN SUMMARY TITLE	HOW I WILL USE MY RECOVERY PROGRAM TO PREVENT OR MANAGE THIS WARNING SIGN

1. _____: _____

2. _____: _____

3. _____: _____

4. _____: _____

5. _____: _____

6. _____: _____

7. _____: _____

#	WARNING SIGN SUMMARY TITLE	HOW I WILL USE MY RECOVERY PROGRAM TO PREVENT OR MANAGE THIS WARNING SIGN

8. _____: _____

9. _____: _____

10. _____: _____

11. _____: _____

12. _____: _____

13. _____: _____

14. _____: _____

15. _____: _____

The Staying Sober Workbook by Terence T. Gorski
Available from: Independence Press, P.O. Box HH, Independence, MO 64055

Exercise 29

Name: _____

Week beginning: _____

WEEKLY PLANNING GUIDE

	Monday	Tuesday	Wednesday	Thursday	Friday	Saturday	Sunday
7-8 AM							
8-9 AM							
9-10 AM							
10-11 AM							
11-12 AM							
12-1 PM							
1-2 PM							
2-3 PM							
3-4 PM							
4-5 PM							
5-6 PM							
EVENING							

The Staying Sober Workbook by Terence T. Gorski
Available from: Independence Press, P.O. Box HH, Independence, MO 64055

Exercise 29

Name: _____

Week beginning: _____

WEEKLY PLANNING GUIDE

	Monday	Tuesday	Wednesday	Thursday	Friday	Saturday	Sunday
7-8 AM							
8-9 AM							
9-10 AM							
10-11 AM							
11-12 AM							
12-1 PM							
1-2 PM							
2-3 PM							
3-4 PM							
4-5 PM							
5-6 PM							
EVENING							

The Staying Sober Workbook by Terence T. Gorski
Available from: Independence Press, P.O. Box HH, Independence, MO 64055

Exercise 29

Name: _____

Week beginning: _____

WEEKLY PLANNING GUIDE

	Monday	Tuesday	Wednesday	Thursday	Friday	Saturday	Sunday
7-8 AM							
8-9 AM							
9-10 AM							
10-11 AM							
11-12 AM							
12-1 PM							
1-2 PM							
2-3 PM							
3-4 PM							
4-5 PM							
5-6 PM							
EVENING							

The Staying Sober Workbook by Terence T. Gorski
Available from: Independence Press, P.O. Box HH, Independence, MO 64055

Exercise 29

Name: _____

Week beginning: _____

WEEKLY PLANNING GUIDE

	Monday	Tuesday	Wednesday	Thursday	Friday	Saturday	Sunday
7-8 AM							
8-9 AM							
9-10 AM							
10-11 AM							
11-12 AM							
12-1 PM							
1-2 PM							
2-3 PM							
3-4 PM							
4-5 PM							
5-6 PM							
EVENING							

The Staying Sober Workbook by Terence T. Gorski
Available from: Independence Press, P.O. Box HH, Independence, MO 64055

Exercise 30

PATIENT NAME _____

THERAPIST_____

DATE _____

THE SIGNIFICANT OTHER LIST

Instructions: The first step in developing a relapse intervention network is to develop a list of potential members. In the space provided below put the names of five persons with whom you have regular contact who could become involved in your relapse prevention network. If you have trouble identifying five it may mean you are still socially isolated as a consequence of your addiction.

Person #1: _____

Relationship: _____

Person #2: _____

Relationship: _____

Person #3: _____

Relationship: _____

Person #4: _____

Relationship: _____

Person #5: _____

Relationship: _____

Five copies of Exercise 31: The Significant Other Evaluation Form are included in the exercise manual. Complete one for each person that you have listed here to assure that they are appropriate for involvement in your relapse prevention network. After you complete these exercises be sure to review them with your counselor before inviting anyone to become involved.

The Staying Sober Workbook by Terence T. Gorski
Available from: Independence Press, P.O. Box HH, Independence, MO 64055

Exercise 31
(worksheet #1)

THE SIGNIFICANT OTHER EVALUATION

Instructions: List one person from your Significant Other List and answer the following questions to determine if that person is appropriate for your relapse prevention network.

Person #1: _____

Relationship: _____

1. Does he/she understand chemical dependency as a disease or is he/she willing to learn about it?.. ☐ Yes ☐ No
2. Is he/she supportive of my recovery from addiction by using a program of total abstinence?.. ☐ Yes ☐ No
3. Is this person supportive of relapse prevention planning as part of my recovery program?.. ☐ Yes ☐ No
4. If he/she uses alcohol does he/she drink less than twice per weekly, rarely have more than two regular sized drinks per occasion, and refrain from using any illegal drugs?..... ☐ Yes ☐ No
5. If he/she is a recovering addict, is he/she involved in a recovery program for chemical dependency?.. ☐ Yes ☐ No
6. If he/she is co-dependent, is he/she involved in a recovery program for co-dependency?... ☐ Yes ☐ No
7. Did you discuss the prospect of involving this person with your counselor or sponsor?.... ☐ Yes ☐ No

Please summarize their comments: _____

_____

_____

_____

_____

_____

8. Is he/she appropriate for involvement in my relapse prevention network?............... ☐ Yes ☐ No

   Why is this person appropriate?

   _____

   _____

   _____

   _____

9. Did you ask him/her to become involved?... ☐ Yes ☐ No
10. Did he/she agree to become involved?.. ☐ Yes ☐ No

The Staying Sober Workbook by Terence T. Gorski
Available from: Independence Press, P.O. Box HH, Independence, MO 64055

PATIENT NAME _____

THERAPIST_____

DATE_____

THE SIGNIFICANT OTHER EVALUATION

Instructions: List one person from your Significant Other List and answer the following questions to determine if that person is appropriate for your relapse prevention network.

Person #2: _____

Relationship: _____

1. Does he/she understand chemical dependency as a disease or is he/she willing to learn about it?.. ☐ Yes ☐ No

2. Is he/she supportive of my recovery from addiction by using a program of total abstinence?.. ☐ Yes ☐ No

3. Is this person supportive of relapse prevention planning as part of my recovery program?.. ☐ Yes ☐ No

4. If he/she uses alcohol does he/she drink less than twice per weekly, rarely have more than two regular sized drinks per occasion, and refrain from using any illegal drugs?..... ☐ Yes ☐ No

5. If he/she is a recovering addict, is he/she involved in a recovery program for chemical dependency?.. ☐ Yes ☐ No

6. If he/she is co-dependent, is he/she involved in a recovery program for co-dependency?... ☐ Yes ☐ No

7. Did you discuss the prospect of involving this person with your counselor or sponsor?.... ☐ Yes ☐ No

Please summarize their comments: _____

_____

_____

_____

_____

_____

8. Is he/she appropriate for involvement in my relapse prevention network?............... ☐ Yes ☐ No

Why is this person appropriate?

_____

_____

_____

_____

9. Did you ask him/her to become involved?... ☐ Yes ☐ No

10. Did he/she agree to become involved?... ☐ Yes ☐ No

The Staying Sober Workbook by Terence T. Gorski
Available from: Independence Press, P.O. Box HH, Independence, MO 64055

Exercise 31
(worksheet #3)

PATIENT NAME _____

THERAPIST _____

DATE _____

THE SIGNIFICANT OTHER EVALUATION

Instructions: List one person from your Significant Other List and answer the following questions to determine if that person is appropriate for your relapse prevention network.

Person #3: _____

Relationship: _____

1. Does he/she understand chemical dependency as a disease or is he/she willing to learn about it?.. ☐ Yes   ☐ No

2. Is he/she supportive of my recovery from addiction by using a program of total abstinence?.. ☐ Yes   ☐ No

3. Is this person supportive of relapse prevention planning as part of my recovery program? .... ☐ Yes   ☐ No

4. If he/she uses alcohol does he/she drink less than twice per weekly, rarely have more than two regular sized drinks per occasion, and refrain from using any illegal drugs?..... ☐ Yes   ☐ No

5. If he/she is a recovering addict, is he/she involved in a recovery program for chemical dependency? .... ☐ Yes   ☐ No

6. If he/she is co-dependent, is he/she involved in a recovery program for co-dependency?.... ☐ Yes   ☐ No

7. Did you discuss the prospect of involving this person with your counselor or sponsor?.... ☐ Yes   ☐ No

Please summarize their comments: _____

_____

_____

_____

_____

_____

8. Is he/she appropriate for involvement in my relapse prevention network?............... ☐ Yes   ☐ No

Why is this person appropriate?

_____

_____

_____

_____

9. Did you ask him/her to become involved?... ☐ Yes   ☐ No

10. Did he/she agree to become involved?.. ☐ Yes   ☐ No

The Staying Sober Workbook by Terence T. Gorski
Available from: Independence Press, P.O. Box HH, Independence, MO 64055

Exercise 31
(worksheet #4)

PATIENT NAME _____

THERAPIST_____

DATE_____

THE SIGNIFICANT OTHER EVALUATION

Instructions: List one person from your Significant Other List and answer the following questions to determine if that person is appropriate for your relapse prevention network.

Person #4: _____

Relationship: _____

1. Does he/she understand chemical dependency as a disease or is he/she willing to learn about it?.. ☐ Yes   ☐ No
2. Is he/she supportive of my recovery from addiction by using a program of total abstinence?.. ☐ Yes   ☐ No
3. Is this person supportive of relapse prevention planning as part of my recovery program?.. ☐ Yes   ☐ No
4. If he/she uses alcohol does he/she drink less than twice per weekly, rarely have more than two regular sized drinks per occasion, and refrain from using any illegal drugs?..... ☐ Yes   ☐ No
5. If he/she is a recovering addict, is he/she involved in a recovery program for chemical dependency?.. ☐ Yes   ☐ No
6. If he/she is co-dependent, is he/she involved in a recovery program for co-dependency?... ☐ Yes   ☐ No
7. Did you discuss the prospect of involving this person with your counselor or sponsor?.... ☐ Yes   ☐ No

Please summarize their comments: _____

_____

_____

_____

_____

_____

8. Is he/she appropriate for involvement in my relapse prevention network?............... ☐ Yes   ☐ No

   Why is this person appropriate?

_____

_____

_____

_____

9. Did you ask him/her to become involved?...................................... ☐ Yes   ☐ No
10. Did he/she agree to become involved?.. ☐ Yes   ☐ No

The Staying Sober Workbook by Terence T. Gorski
Available from: Independence Press, P.O. Box HH, Independence, MO 64055

PATIENT NAME _____

THERAPIST_____

DATE_____

THE SIGNIFICANT OTHER EVALUATION

Instructions: List one person from your Significant Other List and answer the following questions to determine if that person is appropriate for your relapse prevention network.

Person #5: _____

Relationship: _____

1. Does he/she understand chemical dependency as a disease or is he/she willing to learn about it?... ☐ Yes ☐ No
2. Is he/she supportive of my recovery from addiction by using a program of total abstinence?... ☐ Yes ☐ No
3. Is this person supportive of relapse prevention planning as part of my recovery program?.. ☐ Yes ☐ No
4. If he/she uses alcohol does he/she drink less than twice per weekly, rarely have more than two regular sized drinks per occasion, and refrain from using any illegal drugs?..... ☐ Yes ☐ No
5. If he/she is a recovering addict, is he/she involved in a recovery program for chemical dependency?... ☐ Yes ☐ No
6. If he/she is co-dependent, is he/she involved in a recovery program for co-dependency?.... ☐ Yes ☐ No
7. Did you discuss the prospect of involving this person with your counselor or sponsor?.... ☐ Yes ☐ No

Please summarize their comments: _____

_____

_____

_____

_____

_____

8. Is he/she appropriate for involvement in my relapse prevention network?............... ☐ Yes ☐ No

   Why is this person appropriate?

_____

_____

_____

9. Did you ask him/her to become involved?.. ☐ Yes ☐ No
10. Did he/she agree to become involved?.. ☐ Yes ☐ No

The Staying Sober Workbook by Terence T. Gorski
Available from: Independence Press, P.O. Box HH, Independence, MO 64055

PATIENT NAME _____

THERAPIST_____

DATE_____

THE SIGNIFICANT OTHER WORKSHEET

1. **Name of Significant Other:** _____

2. **Relationship:** _____

3. **Relapse Warning Signs:** What relapse warning signs have you experienced most often when you were around this person in the past? (Select the warning sign from your **Final Warning Sign List.)**

Warning Sign #_____: _____

Did this person cause the warning sign to occur?　☐ Yes　☐ No

Warning Sign #_____: _____

Did this person cause the warning sign to occur?　☐ Yes　☐ No

Warning Sign #_____: _____

Did this person cause the warning sign to occur?　☐ Yes　☐ No

Warning Sign #_____: _____

Did this person cause the warning sign to occur?　☐ Yes　☐ No

Warning Sign #_____: _____

Did this person cause the warning sign to occur?　☐ Yes　☐ No

4. **Effect Upon This Person's Thoughts and Feelings:** What effect did these warning signs have upon the thoughts and feelings of this person?

_____

_____

_____

_____

_____

5. **Past Behavioral Response of the Person:** How did this person behave in response to these warning signs in the past?

_____

_____

_____

_____

6. **Assessment:** How did this person's behavioral response affect your recovery?

☐ It was helpful to my recovery.

☐ It was harmful to my recovery.

☐ It did not help or hurt my recovery.

7. **Rationale for Your Assessment:** Please explain why you assessed this person's response as you did.

_____

_____

_____

_____

8. **Effect Upon Your Thoughts and Feelings:** How did this person's behavioral response to your warning signs affect your thoughts and feelings?

_____

_____

_____

_____

9. **Your Past Behavioral Response to This Person:** What was your past behavioral response to this person's reactions to your warning signs?

_____

_____

_____

_____

10. **Assessment of Your Behavioral Response:** How did your behavioral response to this person's reaction affect your recovery?

☐ It was helpful to my recovery.

☐ It was harmful to my recovery.

☐ It did not help or hurt my recovery.

11. **Rationale for Your Assessment:** Please explain why you assessed your past reaction as you did.

_____

_____

_____

_____

12. **Preferred Way for the Other Person to Respond:** How could this person respond to your warning signs in a way that is more helpful to your recovery?

_____

_____

_____

_____

_____

13. **Denial Interruption Plan:** What do you want the other person to do if, when he or she responds in your preferred manner, you deny that there is a problem and continue to act out the warning signs?

_____

_____

_____

_____

_____

14. **Response to Past Relapse Episodes:** How did this person react in the past when you returned to addictive use?

_____

_____

_____

_____

15. **Relapse Early Intervention Plan:** What do you want this person to do if you return to addictive use in the future?

_____

_____

_____

_____

_____

The Staying Sober Workbook by Terence T. Gorski
Available from: Independence Press, P.O. Box HH, Independence, MO 64055

PATIENT NAME _____

THERAPIST _____

DATE _____

THE SIGNIFICANT OTHER WORKSHEET

1. **Name of Significant Other:** _____

2. **Relationship:** _____

3. **Relapse Warning Signs:** What relapse warning signs have you experienced most often when you were around this person in the past? (Select the warning sign from your **Final Warning Sign List.)**

Warning Sign #_____: _____

Did this person cause the warning sign to occur? ☐ Yes ☐ No

Warning Sign #_____: _____

Did this person cause the warning sign to occur? ☐ Yes ☐ No

Warning Sign #_____: _____

Did this person cause the warning sign to occur? ☐ Yes ☐ No

Warning Sign #_____: _____

Did this person cause the warning sign to occur? ☐ Yes ☐ No

Warning Sign #_____: _____

Did this person cause the warning sign to occur? ☐ Yes ☐ No

4. **Effect Upon This Person's Thoughts and Feelings:** What effect did these warning signs have upon the thoughts and feelings of this person?

_____

_____

_____

_____

_____

_____

5. **Past Behavioral Response of the Person:** How did this person behave in response to these warning signs in the past?

_____

_____

_____

_____

_____

6. **Assessment:** How did this person's behavioral response affect your recovery?

☐ It was helpful to my recovery.

☐ It was harmful to my recovery.

☐ It did not help or hurt my recovery.

7. **Rationale for Your Assessment:** Please explain why you assessed this person's response as you did.

_____

_____

_____

_____

_____

8. **Effect Upon Your Thoughts and Feelings:** How did this person's behavioral response to your warning signs affect your thoughts and feelings?

_____

_____

_____

_____

_____

9. **Your Past Behavioral Response to This Person:** What was your past behavioral response to this person's reactions to your warning signs?

_____

_____

_____

_____

_____

10. **Assessment of Your Behavioral Response:** How did your behavioral response to this person's reaction affect your recovery?

☐ It was helpful to my recovery.

☐ It was harmful to my recovery.

☐ It did not help or hurt my recovery.

11. **Rationale for Your Assessment:** Please explain why you assessed your past reaction as you did.

_____

_____

_____

_____

_____

12. **Preferred Way for the Other Person to Respond:** How could this person respond to your warning signs in a way that is more helpful to your recovery?

_____

_____

_____

_____

_____

_____

13. **Denial Interruption Plan:** What do you want the other person to do if, when he or she responds in your preferred manner, you deny that there is a problem and continue to act out the warning signs?

_____

_____

_____

_____

_____

14. **Response to Past Relapse Episodes:** How did this person react in the past when you returned to addictive use?

_____

_____

_____

_____

_____

15. **Relapse Early Intervention Plan:** What do you want this person to do if you return to addictive use in the future?

_____

_____

_____

_____

_____

The Staying Sober Workbook **by Terence T. Gorski**
Available from: Independence Press, P.O. Box HH, Independence, MO 64055

PATIENT NAME _____

THERAPIST_____

DATE_____

THE SIGNIFICANT OTHER WORKSHEET

1. **Name of Significant Other:** _____

2. **Relationship:** _____

3. **Relapse Warning Signs:** What relapse warning signs have you experienced most often when you were around this person in the past? (Select the warning sign from your **Final Warning Sign List.**)

Warning Sign #_____: _____

Did this person cause the warning sign to occur? ☐ Yes ☐ No

Warning Sign #_____: _____

Did this person cause the warning sign to occur? ☐ Yes ☐ No

Warning Sign #_____: _____

Did this person cause the warning sign to occur? ☐ Yes ☐ No

Warning Sign #_____: _____

Did this person cause the warning sign to occur? ☐ Yes ☐ No

Warning Sign #_____: _____

Did this person cause the warning sign to occur? ☐ Yes ☐ No

4. **Effect Upon This Person's Thoughts and Feelings:** What effect did these warning signs have upon the thoughts and feelings of this person?

_____

_____

_____

_____

_____

_____

5. **Past Behavioral Response of the Person:** How did this person behave in response to these warning signs in the past?

_____

_____

_____

_____

6. **Assessment:** How did this person's behavioral response affect your recovery?

☐ It was helpful to my recovery.

☐ It was harmful to my recovery.

☐ It did not help or hurt my recovery.

7. **Rationale for Your Assessment:** Please explain why you assessed this person's response as you did.

_____

_____

_____

_____

8. **Effect Upon Your Thoughts and Feelings:** How did this person's behavioral response to your warning signs affect your thoughts and feelings?

_____

_____

_____

_____

9. **Your Past Behavioral Response to This Person:** What was your past behavioral response to this person's reactions to your warning signs?

_____

_____

_____

_____

10. **Assessment of Your Behavioral Response:** How did your behavioral response to this person's reaction affect your recovery?

☐ It was helpful to my recovery.

☐ It was harmful to my recovery.

☐ It did not help or hurt my recovery.

11. **Rationale for Your Assessment:** Please explain why you assessed your past reaction as you did.

_____

_____

_____

_____

12. **Preferred Way for the Other Person to Respond:** How could this person respond to your warning signs in a way that is more helpful to your recovery?

_____

_____

_____

_____

_____

_____

13. **Denial Interruption Plan:** What do you want the other person to do if, when he or she responds in your preferred manner, you deny that there is a problem and continue to act out the warning signs?

_____

_____

_____

_____

_____

_____

14. **Response to Past Relapse Episodes:** How did this person react in the past when you returned to addictive use?

_____

_____

_____

_____

_____

_____

15. **Relapse Early Intervention Plan:** What do you want this person to do if you return to addictive use in the future?

_____

_____

_____

_____

_____

_____

The Staying Sober Workbook **by Terence T. Gorski**
Available from: Independence Press, P.O. Box HH, Independence, MO 64055

**Exercise 32
(worksheet #4)**

PATIENT NAME _____

THERAPIST_____

DATE_____

THE SIGNIFICANT OTHER WORKSHEET

1. **Name of Significant Other:** _____

2. **Relationship:** _____

3. **Relapse Warning Signs:** What relapse warning signs have you experienced most often when you were around this person in the past? (Select the warning sign from your **Final Warning Sign List.**)

Warning Sign #_____: _____

Did this person cause the warning sign to occur? ☐ Yes ☐ No

Warning Sign #_____: _____

Did this person cause the warning sign to occur? ☐ Yes ☐ No

Warning Sign #_____: _____

Did this person cause the warning sign to occur? ☐ Yes ☐ No

Warning Sign #_____: _____

Did this person cause the warning sign to occur? ☐ Yes ☐ No

Warning Sign #_____: _____

Did this person cause the warning sign to occur? ☐ Yes ☐ No

4. **Effect Upon This Person's Thoughts and Feelings:** What effect did these warning signs have upon the thoughts and feelings of this person?

_____

_____

_____

_____

_____

_____

5. **Past Behavioral Response of the Person:** How did this person behave in response to these warning signs in the past?

_____

_____

_____

_____

6. **Assessment:** How did this person's behavioral response affect your recovery?

☐ It was helpful to my recovery.

☐ It was harmful to my recovery.

☐ It did not help or hurt my recovery.

7. **Rationale for Your Assessment:** Please explain why you assessed this person's response as you did.

_____

_____

_____

_____

_____

8. **Effect Upon Your Thoughts and Feelings:** How did this person's behavioral response to your warning signs affect your thoughts and feelings?

_____

_____

_____

_____

_____

9. **Your Past Behavioral Response to This Person:** What was your past behavioral response to this person's reactions to your warning signs?

_____

_____

_____

_____

_____

10. **Assessment of Your Behavioral Response:** How did your behavioral response to this person's reaction affect your recovery?

☐ It was helpful to my recovery.

☐ It was harmful to my recovery.

☐ It did not help or hurt my recovery.

11. **Rationale for Your Assessment:** Please explain why you assessed your past reaction as you did.

_____

_____

_____

_____

_____

12. **Preferred Way for the Other Person to Respond:** How could this person respond to your warning signs in a way that is more helpful to your recovery?

_____

_____

_____

_____

_____

_____

13. **Denial Interruption Plan:** What do you want the other person to do if, when he or she responds in your preferred manner, you deny that there is a problem and continue to act out the warning signs?

_____

_____

_____

_____

_____

_____

14. **Response to Past Relapse Episodes:** How did this person react in the past when you returned to addictive use?

_____

_____

_____

_____

_____

_____

15. **Relapse Early Intervention Plan:** What do you want this person to do if you return to addictive use in the future?

_____

_____

_____

_____

_____

_____

The Staying Sober Workbook by Terence T. Gorski
Available from: Independence Press, P.O. Box HH, Independence, MO 64055

THE SIGNIFICANT OTHER WORKSHEET

1. **Name of Significant Other:** _____

2. **Relationship:** _____

3. **Relapse Warning Signs:** What relapse warning signs have you experienced most often when you were around this person in the past? (Select the warning sign from your **Final Warning Sign List.)**

Warning Sign #_____: _____

Did this person cause the warning sign to occur?   ☐ Yes   ☐ No

Warning Sign #_____: _____

Did this person cause the warning sign to occur?   ☐ Yes   ☐ No

Warning Sign #_____: _____

Did this person cause the warning sign to occur?   ☐ Yes   ☐ No

Warning Sign #_____: _____

Did this person cause the warning sign to occur?   ☐ Yes   ☐ No

Warning Sign #_____: _____

Did this person cause the warning sign to occur?   ☐ Yes   ☐ No

4. **Effect Upon This Person's Thoughts and Feelings:** What effect did these warning signs have upon the thoughts and feelings of this person?

_____

_____

_____

_____

_____

_____

5. **Past Behavioral Response of the Person:** How did this person behave in response to these warning signs in the past?

_____

_____

_____

_____

_____

6. **Assessment:** How did this person's behavioral response affect your recovery?

☐ It was helpful to my recovery.

☐ It was harmful to my recovery.

☐ It did not help or hurt my recovery.

7. **Rationale for Your Assessment:** Please explain why you assessed this person's response as you did.

_____

_____

_____

_____

8. **Effect Upon Your Thoughts and Feelings:** How did this person's behavioral response to your warning signs affect your thoughts and feelings?

_____

_____

_____

_____

_____

9. **Your Past Behavioral Response to This Person:** What was your past behavioral response to this person's reactions to your warning signs?

_____

_____

_____

_____

10. **Assessment of Your Behavioral Response:** How did your behavioral response to this person's reaction affect your recovery?

☐ It was helpful to my recovery.

☐ It was harmful to my recovery.

☐ It did not help or hurt my recovery.

11. **Rationale for Your Assessment:** Please explain why you assessed your past reaction as you did.

_____

_____

_____

_____

12. **Preferred Way for the Other Person to Respond:** How could this person respond to your warning signs in a way that is more helpful to your recovery?

_____

_____

_____

_____

_____

_____

13. **Denial Interruption Plan:** What do you want the other person to do if, when he or she responds in your preferred manner, you deny that there is a problem and continue to act out the warning signs?

_____

_____

_____

_____

_____

_____

14. **Response to Past Relapse Episodes:** How did this person react in the past when you returned to addictive use?

_____

_____

_____

_____

_____

_____

15. **Relapse Early Intervention Plan:** What do you want this person to do if you return to addictive use in the future?

_____

_____

_____

_____

_____

_____

The Staying Sober Workbook by Terence T. Gorski
Available from: Independence Press, P.O. Box HH, Independence, MO 64055

Name: _____

A CHECK-LIST FOR STARTING
YOUR RELAPSE PREVENTION NETWORK

☐ 1. **Select Potential Members.** Select the potential members for the relapse prevention network by entering their names and relationship to you on the **Significant Other List.**

☐ 2. **Evaluate Potential Members.** Evaluate each potential member by completing a **Significant Other Evaluation** exercise for each person you selected.

☐ 3. **Discuss Your Evaluation.** Discuss the contents of these worksheets with your counselor or fellow AA members who are supportive of your developing a relapse prevention network with the goal of deciding who should be involved in the network.

☐ 4. **Decide Who to Invite.** Decide who you will invite to join.

☐ 5. **First Private Conversation.** Talk with each potential member privately in order to invite them. Do the following in that first private conversation:

  ☐ A. Explain your need for their help in your recovery.

  ☐ B. Explain your recovery and relapse history.

  ☐ C. Make amends to the person for any harm your addiction or your relapse history may have caused.

  ☐ D. Explain that the relapse prevention group will meet three or four times for a period of one and a half to two hours.

  ☐ E. Give the person a blank copy of the **Significant Other Worksheet.** Tell them that you will fill out this worksheet with your ideas and would like to discuss your answers with them in a second private conversation.

  ☐ F. Set the time and the date for the second private conversation.

☐ 6. **Complete Significant Other Worksheets.** Complete a **Significant Other Worksheet** for each person prior to your second private meeting. These worksheets ask you to identify the relapse warning signs you typically experience around that person, how he or she has reacted in the past, and how he or she can react in a more helpful way in the future.

☐ 7. **Second Private Conversation.** In the second private conversation do the following:

  ☐ A. Ask the person if he or she had any reactions to your first conversation. Discuss how he or she thought and felt about your first meeting.

  ☐ B. Review the contents of the **Significant Other Worksheet** with the person.

  ☐ C. Ask if he or she agrees with your assessment.

  ☐ D. Discuss any disagreements and modify the answers on the form as necessary to assure you both understand and are in agreement with each other.

  ☐ E. Invite the person to meet with the other members of the network for a group meeting. Tell them the date, time, and location for the first group meeting.

  ☐ F. Get a firm commitment from them to attend the meeting.

☐ 8. Conduct the first group meeting using the following agenda:

  ☐ A. **Introductions.** Ask all members to introduce themselves and describe why they decided to become involved.

  ☐ B. **Briefly Tell Your Story.** Briefly describe your recovery and relapse history. This should last no longer than 10 minutes.

  ☐ C. **Explain Each Member's Importance.** Describe why you selected each person and why each person is important to your recovery.

  ☐ D. **Briefly Explain the Recovery/relapse Process.** Briefly explain the recovery and relapse process and the steps of relapse prevention planning. If necessary lend them copies of the book *Staying Sober—A Guide to Relapse Prevention* to read.

E. **Review Your Warning Signs with the Group.** Present your personal warning signs of relapse to the group one at a time. After presenting the warning sign, ask if anyone has any questions, has anything to add, or has any problems with what they have heard you say.

F. **Get Feedback from the Members.** After all the personal warning signs have been read, go around the circle and ask everyone to answer three questions:

   (1) Which warning signs do you believe I described correctly?

   (2) Which warning signs do you think I described inaccurately?

   (3) Can you think of any warning signs that should be added to the list?

G. **Closure Exercise.** Ask each member to share with the group their reaction to this session by describing what they learned and how they feel as a result of attending.

H. **Refreshments.** Serve refreshments and socialize briefly.

I. **Adjournment.** Set the time and place for the next meeting and adjourn.

9. **Review and Revise the Significant Other Worksheets.** Review and revise the **Significant Other Worksheets** that you prepared earlier. There probably will be new information that came up in the first session that will change your previous responses.

10. **Conduct the Second Meeting.** Conduct the second meeting using the following agenda:

A. **Reactions to Last Session.** Ask everyone to share their reactions to the last meeting. Go around the circle and ask everyone to comment. Be sure to ask people what they thought about the last meeting and how they felt about what happened.

B. **Review of Significant Other Worksheets.** Review the questions on **Significant Other Worksheets** one by one and discuss in the group.

C. **Keeping Notes.** Keep notes on what you learn from the comments and discussion.

D. **Limit Discussion Time.** Limit the discussion to approximately 90 minutes. If necessary schedule an extra meeting to review all worksheets.

E. **Closure Exercise.** Ask everyone to share with the group their reactions to this session by describing what they learned and how they feel as a result of attending.

F. **Refreshments.** Serve refreshments and socialize briefly.

G. **Adjournment.** Set the time and place for the next meeting and adjourn.

11. **The Third Meeting.** Conduct the third meeting using the following agenda.

A. **Reactions to Last Session.** Ask everyone to share their reactions to the last meeting. Go around the circle and ask everyone to comment. Be sure to ask people what they thought about the last meeting and how they felt about what happened.

B. **Warning Sign Interruption Plan.** Discuss what members are willing to do if you are showing relapse warning signs and refuse to listen to feedback or change your behavior.

C. **Practice at Warning Sign Interruption.** Have the group imagine that you have been showing a relapse warning sign for several weeks and have them pretend to confront you about what is happening. Discuss the strengths and weaknesses of the confrontation after the role play is done. Remember the goal is to be supportive yet directive. The love and the caring must come through along with the rigorous honesty.

☐ D. **Relapse Early Intervention Plan.** Discuss what you want each member to do should you return to addictive use. Work together to design an early intervention plan that will put pressure on you to enter treatment should you return to addictive use.

☐ E. **Practice at Relapse Intervention.** Ask the group to imagine that you have returned to addictive use and they are meeting with you. Have them pretend to intervene upon you and see how well they handle it. Present some resistance or denial just to see how the group handles. Tell the group better ways that they can bypass your denial and pressure you to get into treatment.

☐ F. **Closure Exercise.** Ask each member to share with the group their reaction to this session by describing what they learned and how they feel as a result of attending.

☐ G. **Refreshments.** Serve refreshments and socialize briefly.

☐ H. **Adjournment.** Set the time and place for the next meeting and adjourn.

☐ 12. Establish a follow-up meeting for one month later and a schedule to talk regularly with members at AA meetings, in personal visits, or over the telephone.

The Staying Sober Workbook by Terence T. Gorski
Available from: Independence Press, P.O. Box HH, Independence, MO 64055;

FOLLOW-UP

Instructions: In the space provided below fill in the dates and the method that you are going to use for updating your relapse prevention plan. The method of update is how and with whom you are going to review your relapse prevention plan.

DATE: _____ Method for Update: _____

_____

_____

_____

DATE: _____ Method for Update: _____

_____

_____

_____

DATE: _____ Method for Update: _____

_____

_____

_____

DATE: _____ Method for Update: _____

_____

_____

_____

DATE: _____ Method for Update: _____

_____

_____

_____

DATE: _____ Method for Update: _____

_____

_____

_____

The Staying Sober Workbook by Terence T. Gorski
Available from: Independence Press, P.O. Box HH, Independence, MO 64055

Appendix A

Answer Sheet for Exercise 10: The Relapse Education Self-Test

Part 1: Addictive Disease

1. True
2. False
3. False
4. True

Part 2: Post Acute Withdrawal

5. False
6. True
7. True
8. True
9. True
10. True
11. True

Part 3: Managing Post Acute Withdrawal

12. True
13. False
14. False
15. True
16. True
17. True

Part 4: Phases of Recovery

18. True
19. True
20. False
21. False
22. True
23. True
24. False

Part 5: Relapse Syndrome

25. True
26. True
27. True
28. False
29. False
30. True

Scoring and Interpretation Key for Exercise 22: The Recovery Questionnaire

The following guidelines will help you to interpret the relationship of your basic recovery program to tendency to relapse. If you scored . . .

0 - 25 Points — Lack of recovery-support activities was probably a primary factor in your relapse.

26 - 50 Points — Lack of recovery support activities was probably a strong influence on your past relapse, but there are probably other areas that need to be considered in terms of stressors, problems, and relapse warning signs.

51 - 75 Points — Other problems probably interfered with the effectiveness of your recovery program.

THE QUESTIONNAIRE OF TWELVE STEP COMPLETION

Instructions: The following Questionnaire was constructed from the recommendations contained in the book **The Twelve Steps and Twelve Traditions** published by the Alcoholics Anonymous World Services Office in New York, New York. Refer to this book if you have difficulty understanding the meaning of any question.

Answer each question as honestly as you can. Please use the following definitions in answering each question:

FULL COMPLETION: The task described in the statement was fully completed to my satisfaction.

PARTIAL COMPLETION: The task was started and some progress was made but as of this time it is not fully completed.

NO COMPLETION: The task was never begun or it was attempted but no progress was made.

Step 1: Admitted we were powerless over alcohol, that our lives had become unmanageable.

1. I admitted that the use of alcohol or drugs had caused major problems in my life.

   ☐ Fully Completed (2) ☐ Partially Completed (1) ☐ No Completion (0)

2. I admitted that I was powerless to control the use of alcohol or drugs.

   ☐ Fully Completed (2) ☐ Partially Completed (1) ☐ No Completion (0)

3. I admitted that my life became unmanageable as a result of alcohol or drug use.

   ☐ Fully Completed (2) ☐ Partially Completed (1) ☐ No Completion (0)

4. I admitted that I was powerless to effectively manage my life as long as I continue to use alcohol or drugs.

   ☐ Fully Completed (2) ☐ Partially Completed (1) ☐ No Completion (0)

   STEP 1 Sub-score = _____ (out of a possible 8)

Step 2: Came to believe that a power greater than ourselves could restore us to sanity.

1. I admitted that as a result of my addiction I am suffering from a form of "addiction induced insanity" that creates the obsession and compulsion to use alcohol and other drugs.

   ☐ Fully Completed (2) ☐ Partially Completed (1) ☐ No Completion (0)

2. I came to believe that this "addiction induced insanity" can only be removed with help from outside of myself.

   ☐ Fully Completed (2) ☐ Partially Completed (1) ☐ No Completion (0)

3. I admitted that I have attitudes, beliefs, and rationalizations that block my ability to recognize and accept the help of a power outside of myself.

   ☐ Fully Completed (2) ☐ Partially Completed (1) ☐ No Completion (0)

4. I developed the belief that there is a power greater than myself that can remove the obsession to use alcohol and other drugs.

☐ Fully Completed (2)   ☐ Partially Completed (1)   ☐ No Completion (0)

5. I have started to search for a power outside of myself that has the ability to help me recover from my addiction.

☐ Fully Completed (2)   ☐ Partially Completed (1)   ☐ No Completion (0)

6. I have found a power greater than myself that I believe is capable of removing the obsession and compulsion to use alcohol and other drugs.

☐ Fully Completed (2)   ☐ Partially Completed (1)   ☐ No Completion (0)

STEP 2 Sub-score = _____ (out of a possible 12)

Step 3: Made a decision to turn our will and our lives over to the care of God as we understood Him.

1. I made a decision to accept help from a source outside of myself (my newly found Higher Power).

☐ Fully Completed (2)   ☐ Partially Completed (1)   ☐ No Completion (0)

2. I made a decision to rely upon the principles of the Twelve Step Program to govern the solution to my addiction.

☐ Fully Completed (2)   ☐ Partially Completed (1)   ☐ No Completion (0)

3. I made a decision to rely upon appropriate professional help to assist me in solving other problems that can interfere with sobriety.

☐ Fully Completed (2)   ☐ Partially Completed (1)   ☐ No Completion (0)

4. I made a decision to rely upon the spiritual principles of the Twelve Step Program to govern the actions of my life.

☐ Fully Completed (2)   ☐ Partially Completed (1)   ☐ No Completion (0)

5. I made an active commitment to participate in a structured long-term program of recovery.

☐ Fully Completed (2)   ☐ Partially Completed (1)   ☐ No Completion (0)

6. I came to understand the ideas, principles, and recommendations of the Twelve Step Program.

☐ Fully Completed (2)   ☐ Partially Completed (1)   ☐ No Completion (0)

7. I disciplined myself to review the Twelve Step principles when making important day-to-day decisions.

☐ Fully Completed (2)   ☐ Partially Completed (1)   ☐ No Completion (0)

8. I have learned to recognize where my own ideas and principles are in conflict with those of the twelve steps.

☐ Fully Completed (2)   ☐ Partially Completed (1)   ☐ No Completion (0)

9. I made a decision to act in accordance with Twelve Step principles even when to do so is painful, difficult, or violates my personal ideas, desires, or preferences.

☐ Fully Completed (2)   ☐ Partially Completed (1)   ☐ No Completion (0)

STEP 3 Sub-score = _____ (out of a possible 18)

Step 4: Made a searching and fearless moral inventory of ourselves.

1. I recognized the need to complete a personal inventory of both my strengths and my weaknesses (character defects).

   ☐ Fully Completed (2)   ☐ Partially Completed (1)   ☐ No Completion (0)

2. I recognized and overcame the denial and excuses that blocked me from completing this inventory.

   ☐ Fully Completed (2)   ☐ Partially Completed (1)   ☐ No Completion (0)

3. I selected a knowledgeable and experienced person (an AA sponsor, spiritual advisor, or counselor) to assist in the inventory process.

   ☐ Fully Completed (2)   ☐ Partially Completed (1)   ☐ No Completion (0)

4. I developed a list of questions about my assets (personal strengths) and liabilities (personal weaknesses and character defects) to be used in completing the inventory.

   ☐ Fully Completed (2)   ☐ Partially Completed (1)   ☐ No Completion (0)

5. I completed the inventory by writing a list of my assets (personal strengths) and liabilities (personal weaknesses and character defects).

   ☐ Fully Completed (2)   ☐ Partially Completed (1)   ☐ No Completion (0)

STEP 4 Sub-score = _____ (out of a possible 10)

Step 5: Admitted to God, to ourselves, and to another human being the exact nature of our wrongs.

1. I acknowledged that I was living in isolation from other people and that this isolation prevented me from achieving a comfortable sobriety.

   ☐ Fully Completed (2)   ☐ Partially Completed (1)   ☐ No Completion (0)

2. I acknowledged that my ego (my addictive self) was preventing me from sharing the results of my inventory (my deepest thoughts, feelings, beliefs, and problems) with other people.

   ☐ Fully Completed (2)   ☐ Partially Completed (1)   ☐ No Completion (0)

3. I acknowledged that it was self-defeating to keep the results of my inventory and other distressing and humiliating memories secret by refusing to discuss them with another person.

   ☐ Fully Completed (2)   ☐ Partially Completed (1)   ☐ No Completion (0)

4. I became willing to confide the results of my inventory in another person.

   ☐ Fully Completed (2)   ☐ Partially Completed (1)   ☐ No Completion (0)

5. I selected the person in whom I was willing to confide.

   ☐ Fully Completed (2)   ☐ Partially Completed (1)   ☐ No Completion (0)

6. I discussed the results of my inventory openly and honestly with this person.

   ☐ Fully Completed (2)   ☐ Partially Completed (1)   ☐ No Completion (0)

7. I listened to and accepted advice and direction from the person in whom I confided the results of my inventory.

   ☐ Fully Completed (2)   ☐ Partially Completed (1)   ☐ No Completion (0)

STEP 5 Sub-score = _____ (out of a possible 14)

Step 6: Were entirely ready to have God remove all these defects of character.

1. I acknowledged that, even in sobriety, I am often driven blindly by my desires and character defects into self-defeating behavior with often catastrophic consequences.

   ☐ Fully Completed (2) ☐ Partially Completed (1) ☐ No Completion (0)

2. I acknowledged that I enjoy the temporary pleasure that results from many of my character defects.

   ☐ Fully Completed (2) ☐ Partially Completed (1) ☐ No Completion (0)

3. I identified the character defects that I am ready to give up.

   ☐ Fully Completed (2) ☐ Partially Completed (1) ☐ No Completion (0)

4. I identified the character defects that I am still unwilling to give up.

   ☐ Fully Completed (2) ☐ Partially Completed (1) ☐ No Completion (0)

5. I acknowledged a willingness to give these up at some future time.

   ☐ Fully Completed (2) ☐ Partially Completed (1) ☐ No Completion (0)

6. In moments of prayer and meditation, I asked God to prepare me to take the actions necessary to remove the character defects I am ready to be rid of and make me willing to give up the character defects I still choose to hold on to.

   ☐ Fully Completed (2) ☐ Partially Completed (1) ☐ No Completion (0)

STEP 6 Sub-score = _____ (out of a possible 12)

Step 7: Humbly asked Him to remove our shortcomings.

1. I examined my goals and purposes in life and my means of achieving those goals and purposes.

   ☐ Fully Completed (2) ☐ Partially Completed (1) ☐ No Completion (0)

2. I recognized that character building (psychological growth) and the development of spiritual values are the only meaningful and enduring goals in life.

   ☐ Fully Completed (2) ☐ Partially Completed (1) ☐ No Completion (0)

3. I recognized that my natural desires are merely a means of physical survival, and that physical survival only has meaning and purpose to the extent that it is focused upon developing character and enduring spiritual values.

   ☐ Fully Completed (2) ☐ Partially Completed (1) ☐ No Completion (0)

4. I recognized that I could not live exclusively by my own individual strength and intelligence, but needed help.

   ☐ Fully Completed (2) ☐ Partially Completed (1) ☐ No Completion (0)

5. I recognized the limits of my self-sufficiency by examining the sequence of problems that resulted from an over-reliance upon myself in isolation from others and my higher power.

   ☐ Fully Completed (2) ☐ Partially Completed (1) ☐ No Completion (0)

6. I recognized that humility (the true knowledge of self) is a tool to develop freedom from the bondage of self, and hence provides a means to transcend my current limitations and achieve true and permanent freedom of spirit and peace of mind.

   ☐ Fully Completed (2) ☐ Partially Completed (1) ☐ No Completion (0)

7. I recognized that I could not lead a meaningful and comfortable life without developing a strong sense of humility (a true knowledge of myself including both my strengths and weaknesses).

☐ Fully Completed (2) ☐ Partially Completed (1) ☐ No Completion (0)

8. In prayer and meditation, I asked my Higher Power to remove the defects of character that blocked me from practicing true humility (i.e., acting in accordance with who I really am).

☐ Fully Completed (2) ☐ Partially Completed (1) ☐ No Completion (0)

STEP 7 Sub-score = _____ (out of a possible 16)

Step 8: Made a list of all the persons we had harmed and became willing to make amends to them all.

1. I made an accurate and exhaustive survey of my past life as it affected other people.

☐ Fully Completed (2) ☐ Partially Completed (1) ☐ No Completion (0)

2. I examined this past history to determine where I had been at fault in causing harm to others, or where others had caused me harm.

☐ Fully Completed (2) ☐ Partially Completed (1) ☐ No Completion (0)

3. I wrote down a list of all the persons I had harmed in any way, being especially aware of those that were harmed as a result of my addictive use or the character defects related to my addiction.

☐ Fully Completed (2) ☐ Partially Completed (1) ☐ No Completion (0)

4. I identified the course of action that would be necessary to make amends or restitution to those I had harmed.

☐ Fully Completed (2) ☐ Partially Completed (1) ☐ No Completion (0)

5. I made a list of all the persons I believed had harmed me.

☐ Fully Completed (2) ☐ Partially Completed (1) ☐ No Completion (0)

6. I forgave the wrongs that these others had committed against me.

☐ Fully Completed (2) ☐ Partially Completed (1) ☐ No Completion (0)

7. I examined the consequences of making amends, restitution and communicating my forgiveness to others to discover when to do so would further harm me or others.

☐ Fully Completed (2) ☐ Partially Completed (1) ☐ No Completion (0)

STEP 8 Sub-score = _____ (out of a possible 14)

Step 9: Made direct amends to such people wherever possible, except when to do so would injure them or others.

1. I developed a strong sobriety program that would allow me to maintain sobriety while making amends to others.

☐ Fully Completed (2)   ☐ Partially Completed (1)   ☐ No Completion (0)

2. I determined when and how direct amends could be made to each person in an effective manner.

☐ Fully Completed (2)   ☐ Partially Completed (1)   ☐ No Completion (0)

3. I prepared to approach the amends process with an attitude of quiet sincerity.

☐ Fully Completed (2)   ☐ Partially Completed (1)   ☐ No Completion (0)

4. I initiated the amends process by admitting to others the reality of my alcoholism and the problems it had caused.

☐ Fully Completed (2)   ☐ Partially Completed (1)   ☐ No Completion (0)

5. I completed the amends process by paying or making promises to pay whatever obligations were owed.

☐ Fully Completed (2)   ☐ Partially Completed (1)   ☐ No Completion (0)

STEP 9 Sub-score = _____ (out of a possible 10)

Step 10: Continued to take personal inventory and when we were wrong promptly admitted it.

1. I developed a format for completing a daily inventory that reviewed both my strengths and my weaknesses.

☐ Fully Completed (2)   ☐ Partially Completed (1)   ☐ No Completion (0)

2. I made a commitment to practice this inventory on a daily basis so that it would become an habitual part of my life.

☐ Fully Completed (2)   ☐ Partially Completed (1)   ☐ No Completion (0)

3. I recognized my personal strengths and weaknesses as they became apparent in my daily life.

☐ Fully Completed (2)   ☐ Partially Completed (1)   ☐ No Completion (0)

4. I utilized a personal journal to document the developing pattern of strengths and weaknesses in my life.

☐ Fully Completed (2)   ☐ Partially Completed (1)   ☐ No Completion (0)

5. I made conscious efforts to utilize my strengths in providing service to others.

☐ Fully Completed (2)   ☐ Partially Completed (1)   ☐ No Completion (0)

6. I made conscious efforts to admit my weaknesses and take actions to improve in those areas.

☐ Fully Completed (2)   ☐ Partially Completed (1)   ☐ No Completion (0)

STEP 10 Sub-score = _____ (out of a possible 12)

Step 11: Sought through prayer and meditation to improve our conscious contact with God as we understood Him, praying only for the knowledge of his will and the power to carry that out.

1. I made a decision to believe in a Higher Power and to call that Higher Power God.

☐ Fully Completed (2)　　　☐ Partially Completed (1)　　　☐ No Completion (0)

2. I made a decision to believe that it is possible to develop a personal relationship with the God of my understanding.

☐ Fully Completed (2)　　　☐ Partially Completed (1)　　　☐ No Completion (0)

3. I initiated a daily program of prayer and meditation as an act of faith that such a relationship would develop.

☐ Fully Completed (2)　　　☐ Partially Completed (1)　　　☐ No Completion (0)

4. I focused my prayer and meditation upon receiving a knowledge of God's will for me and the strength to carry that out.

☐ Fully Completed (2)　　　☐ Partially Completed (1)　　　☐ No Completion (0)

5. I was alert for the experiential confirmation that a personal relationship with God was in fact developing and that this relationship was acting to transform my life.

☐ Fully Completed (2)　　　☐ Partially Completed (1)　　　☐ No Completion (0)

6. I experienced a personal transformation as a result of spiritual experiences that confirmed the reality of my Higher Power.

☐ Fully Completed (2)　　　☐ Partially Completed (1)　　　☐ No Completion (0)

7. I acknowledged to myself and others the transformation that had occurred in my life and the role that my relationship with God had played in that occurrence.

☐ Fully Completed (2)　　　☐ Partially Completed (1)　　　☐ No Completion (0)

STEP 11 Sub-score = _____ (out of a possible 14)

Step 12: Having had a spiritual awakening as a result of these steps, we tried to carry this message to alcoholics, and to practice these principles in all our affairs.

1. I recognized that a spiritual awakening had occurred as a result of diligently practicing the previous eleven steps.

☐ Fully Completed (2)　　　☐ Partially Completed (1)　　　☐ No Completion (0)

2. I carried the message of hope and recovery to other suffering alcoholics.

☐ Fully Completed (2)　　　☐ Partially Completed (1)　　　☐ No Completion (0)

3. I made myself available to provide service to those suffering more than I with no expectation of personal reward or compensation.

☐ Fully Completed (2)　　　☐ Partially Completed (1)　　　☐ No Completion (0)

4. I participated in the ongoing recovery process with other alcoholics by attending AA meetings and sharing my experiences, strength, and hope.

☐ Fully Completed (2)　　　☐ Partially Completed (1)　　　☐ No Completion (0)

5. I practiced the principles that underlie these steps in all of my affairs by bringing the spirit of love and tolerance into my family, work life, friendship circles and all aspects of my life.

☐ Fully Completed (2)   ☐ Partially Completed (1)   ☐ No Completion (0)

6. I continued to strive for spiritual progress while avoiding disillusionment with my inability to achieve spiritual perfection.

☐ Fully Completed (2)   ☐ Partially Completed (1)   ☐ No Completion (0)

STEP 12 Sub-score = _____ (out of a possible 12)

Scoring Sheet

STEP 1 Sub-score = _____ of 8

STEP 2 Sub-score = _____ of 12

STEP 3 Sub-score = _____ of 18

STEP 4 Sub-score = _____ of 10

STEP 5 Sub-score = _____ of 14

STEP 6 Sub-score = _____ of 12

STEP 7 Sub-score = _____ of 16

STEP 8 Sub-score = _____ of 14

STEP 9 Sub-score = _____ of 10

STEP 10 Sub-score = _____ of 12

STEP 11 Sub-score = _____ of 14

STEP 12 Sub-score = _____ of 12

TOTAL SCORE = _____ of 152

The Staying Sober Workbook by Terence T. Gorski
Available from: Independence Press, P.O. Box HH, Independence, MO 64055

RELAPSE PREVENTION NATIONAL CERTIFICATION PROGRAM

In 1979 THE CENAPS CORPORATION introduced Relapse Prevention Planning to the Nation. Since then over 120,000 contact hours of training have been provided to more than 10,000 professionals.

Now you can become part of the first National Certification Program for Relapse Prevention Specialists.

Learn the core relapse prevention skills including...

- Stabilization
- Self-assessment
- Relapse education
- Warning sign identification
- Warning sign management
- Recovery planning
- Inventory training
- Involvement of significant others
- Follow-up

Learn how to teach patients to manage common problems that lead to relapse including...

- painful feelings and emotion.
- interpersonal and situational problems.
- problems with judgment and behavioral control

Learn how to prevent relapse by using the principles of...

- proper diagnosis and assessment.
- sentence completion.
- sentence repetition.
- structured inner dialogue.
- image formation techniques.

Learn how to prevent relapse by integrating...

- cognitive restructuring.
- image formation techniques.
- affective restructuring.
- behavioral therapy techniques.
- holistic health principles.

WHO SHOULD ATTEND?

Professionals who are interested in developing expertise in the new area of Relapse Prevention (RP) Therapy. This includes...

- alcoholism and drug dependence counselors,
- social workers,
- psychologists,
- psychiatrists,
- physicians,
- nurses.

The program is designed to help you grow as a clinician, to master the subtleties of relapse therapy, and to successfully collaborate with your colleagues in the practice of relapse prevention.

Participants need to be mature enough to share both professionally and personally. The intensives are not designed for personal therapy, but professional and personal growth cannot be separated. To change professionally we must be willing to change personally. Participants are given that opportunity. People with personal problems that prevent sharing both personal and professional experiences are discouraged from attending.

THE INSTRUCTOR

Terence T. Gorski is the president of The CENAPS Corporation (The Center for Applied Sciences). He holds a Bachelor of Arts degree from Northeastern Illinois University and a Master of Arts Degree from Webster College in St. Louis, Missouri. He is a Senior Certified Addictions Counselor in the State of Illinois.

Mr. Gorski is a nationally recognized speaker, trainer and consultant. He is the author of numerous books and articles including **Learning to Live Again: A Guide to Recovery from Alcoholism; Staying Sober: A Guide for Relapse Prevention; Counseling for Relapse Prevention; and The Management of Aggression and Violence.**

He is a frequent consultant to industry and human service agencies in the United States, and has conducted training workshops in the United States, Canada and Europe. His practical approach to training is based on over 15 years of experience as a therapist, supervisor, program administrator, trainer and consultant.

HOW TO REGISTER

Each class is limited, so apply early. To be accepted, applicants must complete a process that assures they are qualified professionals with basic knowledge of chemical dependency treatment and introductory knowledge of Relapse Prevention Planning.

To receive your application form contact:
Jan Smith, vice-president
The CENAPS Corporation
P.O. Box 184
Hazel Crest, IL 60429
312/335-3606

ORDER FORM

HERALD HOUSE—INDEPENDENCE PRESS
P.O. BOX HH — 3225 SOUTH NOLAND ROAD
INDEPENDENCE, MO 64055

Qty.	Item No.	Item	Price Ea.	Total Price
		Books:		
____	17-0187-8	Understanding the Twelve Steps	$ 12.95	$_____
____	17-0179-7	Recovery Education	$ 3.00	$_____
____	17-0185-1	The Codependent Counselor	$ 11.95	$_____
____	17-0176-2	How to Start Relapse Prevention Support Groups	5.00	_____
____	17-0180-0	The Players and their Personalities (book)	7.00	_____
____	17-0120-7	Staying Sober	10.95	_____
____	17-0136-3	Staying Sober Workbooks	19.95	_____
____	17-0146-0	Staying Sober Exercise Manuals	12.95	_____
____	17-0166-5	Staying Sober Modules*	150.00	_____
____	17-0188-6	Exercise Manual for Modules	7.00	_____
____	17-0105-3	Learning to Live Again	10.95	_____
____	17-0104-5	Counseling for Relapse Prevention	9.95	_____
____	17-0109-6	Family Recovery, Growing Beyond Addiction	6.00	_____
____	17-0164-9	Triad: The Evolution of Treatment	6.00	_____
____	52-2533-7	Passages Through Recovery	6.95	_____
		Brochures:		
____	17-0111-8	The Relapse Dynamic	.10	_____
____	17-0117-7	The Phases and Warning Signs of Relapse	1.00	_____
____	17-0137-1	Mistaken Beliefs	2.00	_____
		Lecture:		
____	17-0165-7	Do Family of Origin Problems Cause Chemical Addiction?	5.00	_____
		Audiocassettes:		
____	17-0156-8	Addictive Relationships	9.95	_____
____	17-0157-6	Cocaine Craving and Relapse	9.95	_____
____	17-0158-4	Understanding Twelve Steps (4 tapes)	36.95	_____
____	17-0139-8	Relaxation by Numbers	7.95	_____
____	17-0140-1	The Phases and Warning Signs of Relapse	7.95	_____
		Adolescent Chemical Dependence:		
____	17-0190-8	Preventing Adolescent Relapse	12.95	_____
____	17-0182-7	Extent of the Problem (Tape)	9.95	_____
____	17-0183-5	Normal Adolescent Development (Tape)	9.95	_____
____	17-0184-3	Understanding Adolescent Recovery and Relapse (2 tapes)	18.95	_____
____	17-0189-4	Adolescent Relapse Warning Signs (booklet)	1.25	_____

TOTAL COST FOR MERCHANDISE $_____

Please add 10% postage and handling. _____

(Missouri residents only add 6.175% sales tax.) _____

TOTAL $_____

RETAIL ORDERS OF $100.00 OR MORE RECEIVE A 20 PERCENT DISCOUNT

Institutions: Please attach a copy of your purchase order. If you have not purchased from Herald House previously, please furnish credit information on the opposite side of this form.

Individuals: Please send check, money order, or credit card information unless you have an established account.

Call toll-free 1-800-767-8181

CREDIT APPLICATION

(Business Accounts)

Name of Company _____

Address _____ City _____ State _____ Zip _____

Telephone _____

ABOUT YOUR COMPANY

    How long in operation? _____

    How long at the above address? _____

    Type of business   _____

    Do you own or lease your building? _____

    Annual sales volume $_____

REFERENCES

    Name of bank   _____

    Address of bank _____

    List three of your suppliers where credit has been established:

    1. Name _____

       Address _____

    2. Name _____

       Address _____

    3. Name _____

       Address _____

Date _____   (Signed)_____

ORDER FORM

HERALD HOUSE—INDEPENDENCE PRESS
P.O. BOX HH — 3225 SOUTH NOLAND ROAD
INDEPENDENCE, MO 64055

Qty.	Item No.	Item	Price Ea.	Total Price
		Addictive Relationships		
____	17-0170-3	Tape 1, The Players and the Personalities	$129.00	$_____
____	17-0171-1	Tape 2, Relationship Styles	$129.00	_____
____	17-0173-8	Tape 3, Relationship Building	$129.00	_____
____	17-0174-6	Three-tape set	$350.00	_____
____	17-0175-4	Preview (three-tape set)	$ 60.00	_____
		An Overview of Recovery and Relapse		
____	17-0129-0	Tape 1, The Bio-Psycho-Social Model of Addictive Disease	$195.00	$_____
____	17-0130-4	Tape 2, The Developmental Model of Recovery	$195.00	_____
____	17-0131-2	Tape 3, The Relapse Process	$195.00	_____
____	17-0132-0	Tape 4, Occupational Relapse Prevention Planning	$195.00	_____
____	17-0133-9	Three-tape set (tapes 1, 2, and 3)	$499.00	_____
____	17-0134-7	Four-tape set	$599.00	_____
____	17-0135-5	Preview (four-tape set)	$ 60.00	_____
		Post Acute Withdrawal		
____	17-0142-8	Part 1: Recognition	$195.00	_____
____	17-0143-6	Part 2: Management	$195.00	_____
____	17-0144-4	The Two-tape Series	$350.00	_____
____	17-0145-2	Preview (two-tape set)	$ 60.00	_____

TOTAL COST FOR MERCHANDISE $_____.
Please add $10.00 postage and handling. _____
(Missouri residents only add 6.175% sales tax.) _____
TOTAL $_____

(No discount on these items)

Institutions: Please attach a copy of your purchase order. If you have not purchased from Herald House previously, please furnish credit information on the reverse side of this form.

Individuals: Please send check, money order, or credit card information unless you have an established account.

Purchase Order No. _____

Ordered by: _____

Phone_____

Bill to _____

Address _____

City _____

State _____ Zip_____

Visa or Mastercard Number _____

Expiration _____

Call toll-free 1-800-767-8181

CREDIT APPLICATION

(Business Accounts)

Name of Company _____

Address _____ City _____ State _____ Zip _____

Telephone _____

ABOUT YOUR COMPANY

How long in operation? _____

How long at the above address? _____

Type of business _____

Do you own or lease your building? _____

Annual sales volume $_____

REFERENCES

Name of bank _____

Address of bank _____

List three of your suppliers where credit has been established:

1. Name _____

    Address _____

2. Name _____

    Address _____

3. Name _____

    Address _____

Date _____ (Signed) _____

ABOUT THE AUTHOR

Terence T. Gorski, M.A., is currently the president of the CENAPS Corporation, a private training and consulting organization in Hazel Crest, Illinois. He has directed alcoholism treatment centers at Ingalls Memorial Hospital in Harvey, Illinois, and Illinois Central Community Hospital in Chicago, Illinois. He has also served as coordinator for an employee assistance program for the Department of the Army at Fort Sheridan, Illinois. He has acted as consultant to numerous national and international treatment programs and is a frequent lecturer at national and state conferences.

Other books by Mr. Gorski are:

Staying Sober: A Guide for Relapse Prevention by Terence T. Gorski and Merlene Miller

Mistaken Beliefs About Relapse by Terence T. Gorski and Merlene Miller

Counseling for Relapse Prevention by Terence T. Gorski and Merlene Miller

Learning to Live Again: A Guide for Recovery from Alcoholism by Merlene Miller, Terence T. Gorski, and David K. Miller

Family Recovery: Growing Beyond Addiction by Merlene Miller and Terence T. Gorski

Brochures and tapes by Mr. Gorski include:

The Relapse Dynamic (the Original Thirty-Seven Warning Signs) by Terence T. Gorski

The Phases and Warning Signs of Relapse by Terence T. Gorski and Merlene Miller

The Phases and Warning Signs of Relapse—the Audio Tape developed by Terence T. Gorski and Merlene Miller; recorded by David K. Miller

To order any of these resources:

Independence Press/Herald Publishing House
P.O. Box HH
3225 S. Noland Road
Independence, MO 64055

Call toll-free: 1-800-767-8181
(Includes Missouri residents)